492 GREAT THINGS ABOUT BEING ITALIAN

492 GREAT THINGS ABOUT BEING ITALIAN

Boze Hadleigh

Skyhorse Publishing

Copyright © 2015 by Boze Hadleigh

All Rights Reserved. No part of this book may be reproduced in any manner without the express written consent of the publisher, except in the case of brief excerpts in critical reviews or articles. All inquiries should be addressed to Skyhorse Publishing, 307 West 36th Street, 11th Floor, New York, NY 10018.

Skyhorse Publishing books may be purchased in bulk at special discounts for sales promotion, corporate gifts, fund-raising, or educational purposes. Special editions can also be created to specifications. For details, contact the Special Sales Department, Skyhorse Publishing, 307 West 36th Street, 11th Floor, New York, NY 10018 or info@skyhorsepublishing.com.

www.skyhorsepublishing.com

10 9 8 7 6 5 4 3 2 1

Library of Congress Cataloging-in-Publication Data is available on file

Cover design by Jane Sheppard
Cover photo credit: Thinkstock

Print ISBN: 978-1-63450-534-5
Ebook ISBN: 978-1-51070-080-2

Printed in China

By the same author:

Holy Cow!
An Actor Succeeds
Celebrity Diss & Tell
Broadway Babylon
Celebrity Feuds!

DEDICATION

To Ronnie and the memory of my Grandmother Leoni

and fond nods to James Sabatino and Enrico Melchiori

ACKNOWLEDGMENTS

As always, grazie mille to Ronnie and to Linda.

Very special thanks to agent Gene Brissie, editor Catherine Kovach, and publicist Sara Winkelman.

Also to acknowledge Connie Becchio, Anthony Bruno, Luciano Mangiafico, Ron Marasco, Joyce Mehess, the late Mario Pei, Anne Salvatore, Mary Stark, the late Gore Vidal, and William Zanghi, Ph.D.

"But who has done more for art and beauty and good cooking than Italy? Name one…."
—*racecar champion Mario Andretti*

"There are two laws in the universe: the law of gravity, and everyone likes Italian food."
—*Neil Simon*

"In a very real sense, Italian culture shaped Europe, and then Europe shaped America."
—*Anne Bancroft (born Anna Maria Italiano)*

"The impact of Rome…every fourth or fifth word of more than one syllable that we speak in English is from Latin."
—*linguist Mario Pei*

"Italian Americans have very much to be proud of, combining these two creative and energetic cultures."
—*Sophia Loren*

INTRODUCTION

The fact that this book's subjects had to be *limited* to 492—as in the year 1492, which would have made this a trilogy—is proof of the overflowing richness of Italy's culture and descendants. After doing all the fascinating research, I'm convinced Italy is one of a handful of nations that has contributed the most to our world.

I could have included yet another artist, another singer or actor, another soccer player, another delicious food or beautiful town, etc. But at who or what else's expense? Again: "only" 492….

Plus it's a book of positives. Here you won't find Al Capone, the Borgias, or Charles Ponzi. Of the far less notorious, the author had to choose whom to omit—not difficult when so many deserve inclusion. Thus, also omitted are a major but particularly anti-Semitic early-Hollywood director, a middle-famous singer known for wife-beating, and a super-famous singer known for his gangster connections and threatening manners. Naturally missing are Mussolini (excepting the inspiration for his first name) and his fascists.

Then there's the question of religion. Most Italians and Italian Americans are Catholics, as is this author's mother (whose mother was a Leoni). There's no separating Italy's history from that of the Church, but although tempted, I omit the current pope, the first one from the Americas—an Argentine Italian—since some might then ask, what about previous popes? Etc. (*Et cetera* is included.)

There's also not a lot here about ancient Rome, most of which was impressive but often negative: dictator Julius Caesar, his great-nephew Augustus who instituted that long line of power-clenching emperors; imperialism and conquest, slavery and gladiators, etc., etc. Besides, ancient Rome is pretty remote from us, excepting the wide-ranging influence of Latin, e.g., *terracotta* ("baked earth"). Also *e.g.*

In this book, non-English and non-Italian words are italicized (*a-ha!*: ital-icized), including those in Latin and French, one of the globe-spanning Latin languages—the author speaks three, among them la bella lingua.

So, caro reader—be you Italian American, half, actually Italian, or none of the above—it is my hope that you'll be entertained and enlightened by this labor of love. I guarantee you'll be surprised, as I was, by the sheer range of Italian contributions, and I am sure anyone with a drop of Italian blood will finish this book even prouder of their heritage.

Viva l'Italia!

Boze Hadleigh
Beverly Hills, CA

L'Accademia di Belle Arte (Academy of Fine Arts) in Florence was Europe's first art school, founded in 1563 specifically to teach the techniques of drawing, painting, and sculpture. Its art collection—the Galleria dell'Accademia—was begun in 1784 to provide subjects for students to study and copy. The gallery includes paintings by Bronzino, Ghirlandaio, Lippi, and Pontormo, but the most notable of the Academy's artworks is Michelangelo's David, one of the two or three most famous statues in the world.

Aida was composed by Giuseppe Verdi to celebrate the opening of the Suez Canal and debuted at Cairo's new opera house in 1871. It's been playing somewhere ever since. Perhaps unintendedly, it was a pioneering interracial love story, for the main male character is Egyptian (Radames, a general) and the main female character is an Ethiopian slave (the daughter of Ethiopia's king). Radames hopes in vain to marry Aida, but the pharaoh's daughter Amneris is in love with him. To make a long opera short, he's accused of treason, sentenced to death, and entombed alive in a temple where his love has already hidden herself, so the two can die in each other's arms.

Alfa Romeo. Most countries produce one or two world-class sports cars. For instance, Germany has the Porsche and Britain has the Jaguar. However, Italy has Alfa

Romeo, Ferrari, Lamborghini, Lancia, and Maserati—all originally separate companies, all but one now owned by FIAT (which also owns Chrysler). Alfa Romeo's history is more complex than its cousins' and originally involved French co-ownership, though from 1932 to 1986 it belonged to an Italian state holding company. The initial name was A.L.F.A.—Anonima Lombarda Fabbrica Automobili, founded in Milan in 1910. One of its Italian investors was surnamed Romeo.

The firm's first racing car bowed in 1913 and Alfa Romeo won the inaugural Grand Prix in 1925. To stay profitable after World War II, the company offered smaller cars as well, and in 1954 introduced the Alfa Romeo Twin Cam engine, in production until 1994. In the 1960s and '70s Alfa Romeo had a run of successful sporty consumer cars and took first prize in several motorsport categories, including Grand Prix motor racing, Formula One, sportscar racing, touring car racing, and rallies. The Alfa Romeo image is *sportif*, deluxe, and Italian high-quality. The company logo—a red cross on the left, a serpent devouring a man on the right—is basically the Milanese coat of arms.

Alfredo sauce was created in the early 1920s by Roman restaurateur Alfredo di Lello for his renowned Fettucine Alfredo. An instant success, it comprised heavy cream, butter, grated Parmesan cheese, salt, and pepper. Subsequent versions may employ egg yolks, flour, and garlic.

Created for pasta, the rich sauce is now also used with chicken, vegetables, and other choices, and is manufactured by numerous concerns, e.g., Newman's Own Alfredo Pasta Sauce.

Amaretti. Amaro means bitter, amaretto is the diminutive. Amaretti (plural) are macaroons made with chopped or ground bitter and sweet almonds mixed with egg whites and sugar. They may have soft centers or be crisp and easily crumbled and used in other desserts. The most coveted amaretti are the elegantly paper-wrapped Amaretti di Saronno.

Amaretto. Amaretto di Saronno, from Saronno in Lombardy, is the most famous but not the sole manufacturer of Amaretto, a liqueur flavored with bitter almonds (also apricot pits). Additionally, it's used to lend a sweetish bitter almond flavor to other drinks and to desserts.

Don Ameche was born Dominic Amici (1908-1993). Although the winner of a Best Supporting Actor Oscar for *Cocoon* (1985), he was best known for the title role in *The Story of Alexander Graham Bell* (1939), an extremely popular biopic of the telephone's alleged inventor. For years, the telephone's nickname was an "Ameche," ironic insofar as the instrument's true inventor may not have been the Scotsman charged with patent fraud, but the Italian Antonio Meucci (see upcoming entry).

If Ma Bell sounds more natural than Ma Meucci, it's mostly due to sheer repetition.

Amerigo Vespucci (1454-1512) couldn't have dreamed that his first name, in feminized form, would become the most famous geographical name—for two continents and one superpower—in modern history. (By contrast, Columbus only got a nation, Colombia (sic), and a federal district (of Columbia) named after him. Also a movie studio.) A Florentine banker, explorer, and cartographer, it was Vespucci and not Columbus who first realized that the lands west of the Atlantic Ocean were separate continents, not the eastern edge of Asia.

(Incidentally, Vespucci, who financed ships sailing to the "Indies," helped supply the beef rations for at least one of Columbus's voyages.)

Manuel I, king of Portugal, invited Amerigo to be an observer on several voyages exploring the east coast of what would become South America. It was on one such voyage that Vespucci discovered the geographical truth, so in 1507 cartographer Martin Waldseemüller proposed that a part of Brazil which Vespucci had explored be named after him: America. The name stuck, and was later applied to all of Brazil, then to the entire southern continent, and eventually to both continents. Fortunately, the German employed the mellifluous "America" rather than "Vespuccia." Viva Amerigo!

Sofonisba Anguissola. Few nonscholars have heard of this female painter from Cremona born in 1532. A pioneer art student at a time when education was largely denied to women and careers considered indecent for married women, she wed twice but followed her work to the royal court in Madrid. Anguissola remained a professional artist until her death at 93 in 1625, back when the average lifespan was much shorter.

Antipasto comes from the Latin for before-the-meal and is intended to awaken the appetite, not satisfy it. Italian homemade meals seldom include an antipasto unless it's a special occasion, though restaurant meals often do. Southern antipasti are simpler than northern ones. Antipasto dishes may be served hot, cold, or room temperature. They use meat sparingly and whole fish almost never, unless small like anchovy or sardines. Stuffed, grilled, or sauteed vegetable dishes are widespread, as are salads. Pasta salads are uncommon in Italy, unlike rice salads. Cold seafood salads are popular.

Michelangelo Antonioni (1912-2007), like Fellini, apprenticed with pioneering neorealist Roberto Rossellini. Previously, Antonioni worked in a bank and reviewed films. Screen success came late, with *L'avventura* (*The Adventure*) in 1960. Antonioni's '60s movies, many starring then-lover Monica Vitti, featured little plot but held audience interest and established his *auteur* reputation. Antonioni's made-in-England *Blow-Up* (1966) was an international hit, but emphatically not so his made-in-the-USA *Zabriskie Point* (1969). Thereafter, smaller budgets, waning health, and a stubbornly sexist perspective diminished the quantity and quality of his output.

The arch. Contrary to popular myth, the Romans didn't invent the arch, which existed in Greece, Egypt, etc. Roman arches were adapted from northern Italy's Etruscan versions.

But pre-Roman arches were used to support smaller structures, like storerooms. With Roman concrete, the empire builders could include arches in bigger and bigger structures, and more often—in everything from amphitheatres (e.g., the Colosseum) and aqueducts to temples and triumphal arches in the Roman Forum.

Architects. Not only Italian painters and sculptors but Italian architects were internationally sought after for centuries. For instance, after Ottoman sultan Mehmet II conquered Constantinople in 1453, he invited architects like Antonio Averlino—known as Filarete—to the renamed Istanbul. The symmetrical lines of Topkapi Palace resemble those of

Milan's Ospedale Maggiori, designed by the Italian. Other invitees included Bologna's Aristotele Fioravanti, who declined and instead headed for Moscow, where he worked on the Kremlin.

Arcimboldo. If you're not sure whether you've viewed his work, you haven't. The most famous paintings of Giuseppe Arcimboldo (1527-1593) are unforgettable. Particularly his Four Seasons series in which the polymath—he was also an architect, scientist, engineer, and stage and costume designer—painted each portrait's head and shoulders from a myriad of each season's fruits and vegetables. Also his reversible paintings which, turned upside-down, change from a bowl of vegetables to *The Vegetable Gardener* or a platter bearing cooked meats becomes a grotesque *The Cook*.

Much of Arcimboldo's career was spent outside Italy, as he served three Hapsburg emperors in a row before being allowed to return to his native Milano.

Argentine Spanish is considered the most musical Spanish in Latin America. Why? It's spoken with an Italian rhythm and emphasis that belie the high percentage of Italian immigration into that country. The Buenos Aires telephone directory contains almost as many Italian surnames as Spanish ones. Italian American actor Guy Williams, born Armando Catalano (see upcoming entry), moved to and died in Buenos Aires during the 1980s. He declared, "I feel more at home and, curiously, more in touch with my roots here than in the U.S. or Italy."

Armani is synonymous with clean, tailored lines in menswear—and with success. In 2001 Giorgio Armani, born in 1934, was pronounced Italy's top designer, achieving sales of $1.6 billion (his personal worth exceeds $8 billion). Originally intended for a medical career, he switched to window dressing, then selling menswear. In 1975 Giorgio and his younger partner (who died in 1985 at 40) launched "Armani," selling clothes out of the front trunk of a VW "Bug." In time, the line added perfumes, accessories, and other luxury goods. Armani's empire numbers 13 factories, almost 5,000 employees, and stores in 36 nations.

The "Michelangelo of Menswear" has also designed costumes for over 100 films (e.g., *The Untouchables*, 1987) and for performers like Italian American Lady Gaga.

In 2008 Armani established a healthy precedent when he banned models with a body mass index below 18, following the death from anorexia nervosa of model Ana Carolina Reston.

Pellegrino Artusi. Rarely do cookbooks have a national importance and sociological impact, but Artusi's 1891 *La Scienza in Cucina e l'Arte di Mangiar Bene* (*The Science of Cookery and the Art of Eating Well*) was such a book. Published three decades after Unification, it was the first cookbook to embrace various regional cuisines as part of a national body. A Tuscan, Artusi favored northern cooking and overlooked many simple foods of the impoverished majority, but he wasn't geographically exclusionary. Besides, he wrote his book in formal Italian, which helped spread the national language at a time when more and more people were learning to read and write Italian while using their own dialect at home.

Arugula the salad vegetable (known in Britain as rocket) was little known outside Italy until the 1980s, when it became trendy. The name reportedly originated in the 1970s, via Italian emigrants, specifically restaurateurs, using the southern Calabrian dialect aruculu (also arucula). As for rocket, it derives from the peppery plant rucola, the diminutive of ruca, meaning rocket!

Charles Atlas appeared in one of the longest and most famous print-ad campaigns ever, promising to turn the proverbial "97-pound weakling" into an envied muscleman like himself. Most Americans had no idea that Atlas was born Angelo Siciliano (1892-1972) in Acri, Calabria. His new surname derived from his shoulders seeming able to uphold the globe, like the mythical Atlas. The top muscleman of his time, Atlas brought bodybuilding into the mainstream and founded his own company in 1929. It's still marketing a fitness program for that 44-kilogram "weakling."

Frankie Avalon. Born Avallone in 1940 in Philadelphia, Frankie played trumpet on TV at 11, opted for singing, then scored a monster hit in 1959 with "Venus." Most of his hits were written and/or produced by Bob Marcucci. When Avalon turned to acting, he renewed his fame in the mid '60s as half of Frankie and Annette, teen fans' favorite screen couple. He and Annette Funicello romped—chastely—through beach movies like *Beach Party*, *Beach Blanket Bingo*, and *How to Stuff a Wild Bikini*. In 1978 Frankie dazzled as Teen Angel in the hit musical *Grease,* and in 1987 he reteamed with Annette in *Back to the Beach*.

Awards. Italy's major entertainment awards are the David di Donatello Award for motion pictures, the Premio (Prize) Regia Televisiva for television, the Premio Ubu for the stage, and the Sanremo Music Festival.

In 2013 Gina Lollobrigida auctioned off her 1956 David di Donatello Award by jeweler Bulgari (given for her performance in *Dangerous But Beautiful*) via Sotheby's. The move was controversial—unlike the concurrent auctioning of her jewels, which fetched almost $5 million—insofar as that particular film award was now historic.

Kaye Ballard (*née* Balotta) is best known for her hilarious—stereotypical, yet with heart and truth—Italian American characterizations on TV as costar of *The Mothers-in-Law* (produced by Desi Arnaz) and supporting actress on *The*

Doris Day Show. She was in too few movies, like *The Ritz* and *Freaky Friday*. Ballard, an accomplished singer and Broadway star, has continued performing for charity, often on behalf of PETA—People for the Ethical Treatment of Animals—into her late eighties.

Back when she was introduced to Frank Sinatra, she proffered a cheery, "Eh, paisan!" to which he coolly replied, "I'm an American."

Baloney. First, as some tourists have discovered, if one visits Bologna, Italy, and asks for bologna or "baloney" meat, it means nothing. Eventually one may be given mortadella, the local sausage made from beef, pork, chicken, turkey, venison, or even soy protein. Second, it was Oscar Mayer who anglicized bologna into baloney, and in the USA October 24 is National Bologna Day—spelled right, but of course mispronounced.

Baloney! A perfectly good word of Italian derivation unfortunately superseded by the Anglo-Saxon expletive that's often preceded by bull. The slang word from the name of an Italian city famous for its sausage that came to mean nonsense (or horsefeathers, etc.) was popularized in the 1930s by Alfred E. Smith, four-time governor of New York and the first Catholic major-party nominee to run for president, in 1928 on the Democratic ticket. Smith often used "baloney" to refer to the bureaucracy in Washington, D.C. (that he hoped to join).

Balsamic oil. The genuine article's full name is Aceto Balsamico di Modena—Balsamic Oil of Modena (balsamic referring to the balsam-like aroma). This condiment has been known in Modena and Reggio Emilia for centuries. Ironically, it took an American to make it popular throughout Italy and the rest of Europe. In 1976 Chuck Williams offered it for sale at his Williams-Sonoma kitchen specialty store in San Francisco after bringing samples back from Italy. The following year it was offered in his national catalogue, which elicited the interest of Italian American restaurateurs, which piqued the interest of Italian chefs, which…anyhow, now it's globally known.

Actually not a vinegar, it's made primarily from must of the white Trebbiano di Castelvetro grape, traditionally slowly boiled down to a half or third its initial volume. Various aging processes then take place, and though not labor-intensive, the product is expensive to produce. A small bottle of true Aceto Balsamico Tradizionale di Modena costs $100 to $500 or more.

Balsamic vinegar. Italy now produces four kinds of balsamic vinegar: the traditional, via the historic methods of Modena; commercially manufactured vinegar in the Modena style; younger versions of Modena-style vinegars; and imitation balsamic vinegar, mostly made in the South. The best vinegars are labeled "da bere" (for drinking), though the cost makes this impractical. Lesser vinegars are "da condire" (for dressing).

In centuries past, balsamico was necessarily precious—no modern methods were available—and the rich used it medicinally (it was believed powerful enough to repel plague) and as a flavor enhancer: a few drops to dress a fruit or augment a sauce. Today it's employed more liberally, in salads and on grilled meats and fish, dribbled over vanilla ice cream, sliced pears or oranges, on strawberries, with crushed raspberries and rocket (an edible Mediterranean relative of the cabbage, used in salads or with certain fruits), or, as some Italians do, added in droplets to chunks of Parmesan cheese after a special meal.

Anne Bancroft. Who would have guessed she was born Anna Maria Italiano (1931-2005)? Or that she'd marry and stay married to Mel Brooks? Or that she would spend six years doing bit and minor roles in movies before taking to the stage for five years and eventually finding Broadway stardom in *The Miracle Worker*, whose 1962 screen version earned her the Academy Award and made her what she remained for the rest of her life, a movie star?

Banquet fit for a queen. Among the most lavish banquets ever seen in Italy was one in 1668 during a visit to Rome by Christina, Sweden's monarch. The incentive was to convert the royal Protestant to Catholicism; her father, a king, had been a champion of Protestantism in the Thirty Years' War. Though she was no *gourmande* and ate little of the sumptuous and varied dishes, the queen appreciated the symbolism and design of the lavish table settings and treasured the watercolor sketches made for her illustrating the trionfi—elaborate sugar sculptures commissioned from such artists as Bernini—that were part of the resplendent display.

Joseph Barbera was half of Hanna-Barbera, a tremendously successful animation studio that won seven Academy Awards and eight Emmy Awards. (William Hanna's background was Irish.) Barbera (1911-2006) spent 70 years in cartoons, as an animator, storyboard artist, cartoon artist, director, and producer. His mother was from Sicily, his father of Lebanese extraction. Born in Little Italy, Joseph grew up speaking Italian. His father, a gambler, abandoned the family when Joseph, the eldest of three boys, was 15. Joseph's maternal uncle became his surrogate father. Younger brother Larry later participated in the WWII liberation of Sicily.

It was at MGM's cartoon unit that Barbera met Hanna. Best known there for Tom and Jerry, in 1957 the pair established their own studio. The rest is animation history, including *The Flintstones*, *The Jetsons*, *Yogi Bear*, *Huckleberry Hound*, *Top Cat*, *The Smurfs*, *Scooby-Doo*, etc., etc.

La Befana is Italy's post-goddess version of Santa Claus or Father Christmas. A toothless old peasant woman who rides a donkey but sometimes flies on a broomstick, she climbs down chimneys on January 6 and distributes presents to good children, typically stocking fillers like small toys and sweets such as befanini—sugar cookies in the shape of alphabet letters. Naughty children receive lumps of garlic mixed with licorice that resemble coal. Where some Americans leave milk and cookies out for Santa, some Italians leave a bit of supper for la Befana and a carrot or apple for her donkey.

Befana is a corruption of the Greek *epifania*, or epiphany.

Bel Paese, meaning beautiful country, is a soft, mild cow's milk cheese from Lombardy, widely popular across Western Europe. Though created in 1929 by Egidio Galbani, the cheese is named for a children's photography book written by Galbani's friend Antonio Stoppani, whose picture still adorns the wrapper.

La bella figura. Better-looking than most nationalities, Italians are known for dressing with flair, often with a casual elegance that may have to do with a high-quality made-in-Italy accessory. Gianni Versace felt, "La bella figura is more than trying to look good, it is grooming and pride…showing others the best of yourself so you both feel good." Gina Lollobrigida defines it as "being in style, your own style, not following the fashion." Luciano Pavarotti explained, "It is our Italian attitude of finding beauty in simple and simply beautiful things. Like our plum-shaped tomatoes. Before you eat one, enjoy its shape and color, its fragrance and texture."

Belladonna is a poisonous member (*Atropa belladonna*) of the deadly nightshade family that contains atropine, sometimes employed as an antispasmodic drug. Thus, belladonna was long used as a muscle relaxant and against menstrual pain, also as an anesthetic; it was called "twilight sleep" when used in childbirth. It was also believed to be effective against motion sickness and peptic ulcers, and to enable witches to fly to their meetings.

On the negative side, women—ergo its name, "beautiful woman"—were encouraged to use belladonna's juice to dilate their eyes, lending a supposedly seductive look. Its side effects were blurred vision and an inability to focus, while long-term use could result in blindness. All the parts of belladonna are toxic—berries, leaves, roots—and ingesting two to five berries is probably lethal.

Non-poisonous members of the nightshade family family include potatoes, tomatoes, eggplants, tobacco, and chili peppers.

Bellini cocktail. It was created at Harry's Bar in the 1930s but not named until 1948, to honor Renaissance artist Giovanni Bellini, whose work was being exhibited in Venice that year. The cocktail is one part fresh white peach nectar (elsewhere, peach puree may be substituted) to two parts Prosecco sparkling wine, poured into a chilled glass—at Harry's it's a slender, not very tall glass; elsewhere it's usually a champagne tulip glass.

Jean-Paul Belmondo. France's top three male movie stars of the 1960s and into the '70s all had Italian antecedents—Yves Montand, Alain Delon, and Jean-Paul Belmondo, whose father Paul, of Italian origin, was a successful sculptor. Jean-Paul, who had a brief boxing career, broke through as an actor with the 1959 New Wave classic *Breathless*, and in several films did his own, often dangerous stunts. "My Italian grandparents would die of vergogna (shame) if I asked, 'Please, Mr. Stuntman, do the hard work for me.'" Born in 1933, the lazy-seeming charmer's films include *That Man From Rio*, *Borsalino*, *Le Guignolo* (a Franco-Italian comedy), and *I Piccioni di Piazza San Marco* (*The Pigeons of St. Mark's Square*).

Belmondo's costar in *Borsalino* (1970) was Alain Delon, whose grandfather came from the once-Italian island of Corsica. Ruled by Genoa from 1282, Corsica was a republic from 1755 to 1769, before being permanently incorporated into France in 1769.

Benetton began in the 1950s as a home business selling colorful knitwear before it moved into cotton and denim. Three brothers and a sister owned and ran the enterprise, which besides youth-targeted clothing (advertised in often catchy, controversial ads) was in the business of acquisition. The group bought a third of the corporation that operates Italy's highways and two-thirds of a highway restaurant chain that includes supermarkets, several Italian airports, and an auto racing team. *Forbes* magazine places the siblings' collective worth at over $10 billion.

Benito Juarez, a native Zapotec and former shepherd, became, against all odds, Mexico's president in 1861. The idealistic reformer is widely considered that country's greatest leader. Who can ever know how their kid will turn out, but at least the parents of a future Fascist dictator (from 1922 to 1945) were informed and open-minded enough to name baby Mussolini after a progressive foreign pioneer.

Tony Bennett. Like the Energizer Bunny, Anthony Dominick "Tony" Benedetto (born 1926) goes on and on. Born in Astoria, New York, he's excelled in most musical genres and received more acclaim and success during the second half of his career. His first hit, "Because of You," was in 1951, and he recorded his signature song, "I Left My Heart in San Francisco," in 1962. Bennett, who's also a successful painter as Anthony Benedetto, has won 17 Grammys, sold some 50 million records, and is known in showbiz circles as Tony Benefit because of his willingness to make charity appearances.

Frank Sinatra opined, "For my money, Tony Bennett is the best singer in the business."

Ingrid Bergman (1915-1982) was one of Hollywood's biggest stars but grew tired of playing only "good girls" and hoped to return to Europe for better roles and films. The Swede was bowled over by Roberto Rossellini's neorealist *Rome: Open City* and wrote him saying she'd like to work with him. They met, fell in love, and left their respective spouses. Bergman was denounced in the U.S. Congress, and her non-Hollywood movies, starting with *Stromboli* (1950), were unofficially banned from American cinemas. Several of her films with Rossellini are now considered classics. In Italy the couple had three children, including actress Isabella Rossellini.

Bergman won a surprise second Oscar (out of three) in 1957 for the 1956 hit *Anastasia*, and marked her return to Hollywood at the 1958 Academy Awards ceremonies, where she presented the award for Best Picture and received a warm standing ovation.

Gianlorenzo Bernini is generally considered, with Michelangelo, the greatest sculptor of the Common Era. The Neapolitan artist (1598-1680), according to historian and former U.S. Consul General in Palermo, Luciano Mangiafico, "infused his sculpture with a dynamic tension, physiological depth, energetic sense of movement, and delicacy of finish unmatched ever since." Most of his sculptures are in Rome, including the Fountain of the Four Rivers in Piazza Navona, but Bernini was also a celebrated painter and architect. He designed St. Peter's Square, the *Baldacchino* in St. Peter's, and the Vatican's Royal Stairway.

Louis XIV hired Bernini to design an extension of the Louvre palace in Paris but then had Versailles built instead.

Roberto Biaggio, one of Italy's all-time soccer greats, was born in Caldogno in 1967. Colorful but modest, idolized yet low-key, he was noted for "il divin codino," his trademark ponytail. Roberto was the only Italian to score in three World Cups (1990, 1994, 1998) and was the fourth-highest goal scorer for his national team. At the club level he was one of three top-scoring Italians in all competitions and shared the record for the most goals scored in World Cup tournaments for Italy.

Post-retirement Biaggio, a longtime Buddhist, became a human-rights activist. In 2002 he was nominated Goodwill Ambassador of the Food and Agriculture Organization of the United Nations and in 2010 earned the Man of Peace Award from the Nobel Peace Prize Laureates. In 2003 he won the inaugural Golden Foot award and in 2011 entered the Italian Football Hall of Fame.

The Biblioteca Ambrosiana became, in 1609, the second library on earth (after that of Oxford University) to open to the general public and place books on shelves instead of chaining them to reading desks. It was founded in Milan and named after the city's patron saint by Cardinal Federico Borromeo, whose agents had sought out books and manuscripts across western Europe and part of the Middle East. Some of the book lover's acquisitions comprised entire libraries, e.g., the manuscripts of the Benedictine monastery of Bobbio (in 1606) and the library of Padua's Vincenzo Pinelli (over 800 manuscripts). The most treasured of the Ambrosiana's 30,000 manuscripts: the *Codex Atlanticus*, 1,119 pages of Leonardo da Vinci's notebooks. The French requisitioned them during Napoleon's occupation—after 1815 they were only partly returned.

Bicycle Thief. The Italian title, *Ladri di Biciclette*, is a double plural. Vittorio De Sica's film is singular and on most critics' ten-best-ever lists—a simple yet emotionally compelling story about a boy and his father, a working man whose crucial bicycle is stolen. In 1948 the government distributor planned to release the film only in Rome and grant it a short run. Italian-film historian Mary P. Wood explained, "The left-wing producer Alfredo Guarini was influential in ensuring its success, re-launching it with personal presentations by De Sica in all the main cities." Popular actor De Sica had formed his own production company and had become a brilliant neorealist filmmaker.

Fortunately, the movie was not only financially successful in a crowded market but earned critical raves and won prizes for best director, screenplay, subject, photography, and music at the Venice Film Festival. It thus drew international interest and didn't take years or decades to be recognized as a timeless and universal classic.

Biscotti means twice-cooked, which was handy pre-refrigeration, as drier food kept longer (twice-baked breads were a staple for the Roman Legions). Biscotti, the plural of biscotto, originated in Prato, Tuscany, and go back several centuries. Oblong almond biscuits (in the U.K.) or cookies (in the U.S.), they're made dry and crunchy by cutting the loaf of dough while it's hot and fresh from the oven. Made of flour, sugar, eggs, and almonds or pine nuts, they're often called cantuccini, especially in Argentina. Variations include pistachios or hazelnuts and spices like cinnamon or anise.

Being dry, biscotti are usually served with a drink or dunked in one. In Italy they're preferred after dinner, often with a Tuscan fortified wine called vin santo.

Robert Blake was born Michael James Vincenzo Gubitosi, in 1933 in New Jersey. His father's first name was Giacomo, his mother's maiden name was Cafone. At five he joined the *Our Gang* cast. His juvenile stage name was changed from Mickey Gubitosi to Bobby Blake. Though Italian American, Robert was often cast as Hispanic or "Indian" (Native American). His big break was the 1967 film of Truman Capote's *In Cold Blood*, but stardom eluded him until the '70s TV series *Baretta*.

He'd auditioned to play Sonny in *The Godfather* and declined to play Ratso Rizzo in *Midnight Cowboy*.

Giovanni Boccaccio (1313-1375), the son of a Florentine banker in Paris, was sent to Naples at age ten to learn banking. Instead, he eventually took up writing and apparently had a five-year affair with a young noblewoman who died of the Black Death, as did his father. Boccaccio then focused on his writing and produced *The Decameron*, 100 short stories cleverly puncturing contemporary pomposity and hypocrisy, not sparing politicians or the Church, and cutting across class lines. Though Boccaccio also wrote much poetry and several other books in Latin and Italian, his name remains synonymous with his *Decameron*.

The title comes from ancient Greek *deca*, meaning ten, and *hemera*, meaning day, since the 100 stories were supposedly recounted over ten days.

Bologna's citizens often refer to their city as "la grassa, la dotta, la rossa"—the fat, the learned, the red. This refers to the city's tempting food (stuffed pastas like tortellini are local specialties, as are lasagna alla bolognese and Bologna's sausages), to its university (claimed to be the oldest in Europe, with over 100,000 students and some two dozen free university museums), and to Bologna as headquarters of Italy's Communist party. For the visitor, this northern city is very centrally located. To the west is Modena, to the north Ferrara, to the east Ravenna, to the south is Florence.

Bologna's stone towers were the skyscrapers of their day and are still impressive and oddly contemporary. At the time, they weren't unique. Wealthy medieval families built high towers to barricade themselves in during civic unrest, and the taller the tower, the greater the family's prestige. Eventually most city governments razed such towers, as in Florence. But of Bologna's 100 or so twelfth-century towers, some 30 remain. The tallest, at 301 feet (91.7 meters), is the Torre degli Asinelli, built in 1109-1119 by the Asinelli family. The tower, which leans about seven feet from vertical, may be climbed via 498 internal steps.

Historically challenged visitors sometimes think the rectangular monochromatic towers are giant modern sculptures.

Bolognese, or alla Bolognese, means Bologna-style. In North America spaghetti bolognese means with meatballs. Bolognese sauce often refers to a robust, long-simmered meat and vegetable sauce called ragu, served with pasta. According to culinary author John Mariani, "A traditional bolognese sauce contains ground pork, beef, pancetta, garlic, tomatoes, vegetables, and, often, mushrooms and/or chicken livers."

The boot. Geographically, Italy is unique. No other country on earth is so clearly shaped like a particular object as the Italian peninsula, which to most any eye resembles a boot—in Italian, lo stivale, the boot! Director Liliana Cavani observed, "Most nations on the map look like pieces of a (jigsaw) puzzle. Ordinary. Undefined. With Italy, you are really looking at something."

"It dangles in the Mediterranean…a nice place to be," quipped comic actor Toto, "but it is kicking Sicily. Too symbolic, no? But still, the boot, a beautiful, elegant shape." Gianni Versace put it another way: "The toe of the Italian boot is aimed at Sicily, a symbol of a soccer ball. No doubt this will give Italy another World Cup victory."

Borromeo Palaces. The Borromeo family built their much better homes and gardens on the Borromean Islands, which they've owned since the 1500s, in the Borromean Gulf, the most beautiful corner of Lake Maggiore. Palazzo Borromeo on Isola Bella (Beautiful Island) is enhanced by ten tiers of terraced gardens and a shell-encrusted grotto, while the English-style gardens on Isola Madre (Mother Island) are home to a flock of white peacocks. This older palace includes a neoclassical puppet theatre created by the set designer of La Scala. The Borromeo palaces are now prime tourist destinations.

Borsalino is an Italian hat company founded in 1857 by Giuseppe Borsalino and best known for fedoras made from

Belgian rabbit fur. It also manufactures other hats, ties, watches, perfumes, clothing, old-fashioned bicycles, and motorcycle helmets.

Borsalino was a 1974 gangster flick starring Jean-Paul Belmondo and Alain Delon (both have Italian antecedents) that featured the famous hats and had a 1974 sequel, *Borsalino and Co*.

Borsalino is also a name applied to Admiral Kizaru in Japanese manga and anime.

Mario Botta is a hip architect with a penchant for right angles and the color pink. Born in 1943 in Mendrisio in Italian-speaking Switzerland, Botta's *oeuvre* includes the Kyobo Tower in Seoul, San Francisco's Museum of Modern Art, the 12-story casino in Campione d'Italia, a pink-brick office block in downtown Lugano nicknamed the Cherry Building after a cherry tree planted on its roof, and the roof of Lugano's bus station, illuminated at night in light pink. Botta also oversaw the restoration of La Scala and designed a cable car and lookout above Locarno, Switzerland.

Botticelli was born Alessandro Filipepi (ca. 1445-1510). Elder brother Giovanni, a pawnbroker, was nicknamed Botticello, meaning little barrel—two such are *botticelli*. Initially apprenticed to a goldsmith, Sandro preferred painting and transferred to Filippo Lippi's studio. He later worked with Verrocchio and Leonardo, who deprecated his rival's landscapes. Botticelli painted some of the Sistine Chapel but is most famous for his beautiful faces and polytheist-inspired compositions. His two masterpieces are *The Birth of Venus* and *La Primavera* (*Spring*).

In the late 1490s Botticelli fell under the spell of the bigoted monk Savonarola and became a fanatic himself, eschewing painting and turning into a censorious prude. Thought to have become partially deranged, he helped collect "immoral paintings"—such as he'd once done—to be publicly burned in the original "bonfires of the vanities."

Chef Boyardee was born Ettore (later Hector) Boiardi in Piacenza in 1897 and arrived in the U.S. with his parents in 1914. In 1924 he opened a restaurant named Il Giardino d'Italia (The Garden of Italy) in Cleveland. Patrons often requested his recipe for spaghetti sauce. In 1928 he started his own company featuring spaghetti sauce and canned pasta. Proud of his heritage, he retained his surname but respelled it "Boy-Ar-Dee"—later "Boyardee."

His canned products ranged from Beef Ravioli, Spaghetti and Meatballs, and Cannelloni to Beefaroni, Twistaroni, Mini Bites, and Mini Os. Boiardi became famous via TV ads and his smiling face on his cans. He died worth a reported $60 million in 1985 in Parma, Ohio.

Bread. "Good as bread"—Buono come il pane—is a traditional Italian way of describing something or someone very special. Anyone who's eaten any of Italy's myriad kinds of breads knows they're special. Yet before the second century B.C.E. when the Greeks taught the Romans how to make bread, there was instead a mush named *puls*, made from farro or spelt, similar to a pre-corn polenta.

The Roman empire depended largely on Egypt for wheat, and during the barbarian invasions when it was unavailable, bread was made from beans, acorns, or other grains. After Rome lost Egypt to the Byzantine empire, breadmaking declined. Not until the late Middle Ages did bread become widely available again in Italy, and even then most bread was made with non-wheat flours. According to *The Dictionary of Italian Food and Drink*, "The distinction between the rich and the poor for much of Italy's history, right into the 20th century, was the difference between those who ate white bread and those who ate dark."

Bread II. A brief sampling of Italian breads:

Pan di miglio—brioche-type bread made with millet flour or cornmeal.

Pan di ramerino—bread flavored with rosemary, from Tuscany.

> Pane casareccio—big bread loaf with a thick crust (means rich-house bread).
>
> Pane del sabato—sabbath bread loaf enriched with eggs, similar to challah.
>
> Pane di Terni—light-crusted, hole-filled saltless bread from Terni in Umbria.
>
> Pane integrale—whole wheat bread, usually in sandwich loaf form (from Latin *integer*—whole).
>
> Pane nero—made with rye and whole wheat flour (from Latin *niger*—black).
>
> Pane pugliese—big bread loaf with rustic texture and hard crunchy crust, from Apulia.
>
> A panetteria or panficio is a specifically bread bakery. A panino is either a round roll or a sandwich made with it. And breadsticks are most associated with which cuisine?

Breaking Away (1979) was nominated for a Best Picture Academy Award and won Best Original Screenplay for Steve Tesich. The coming-of-age story turns on Dave (Dennis Christopher), a typical American high school graduate semi-obsessed with competitive bicycle racing—a big sport in Italy—who loves Italian music and culture. This is all to the semi-horror of his father (Paul Dooley), who tries to ban foods ending in – ini from the house. Cinzano's bicycle team features in the dramatic racing climax. By film's end Dave has learned a life lesson or two, but after meeting an attractive student from France in college, he transfers his cultural interests to French culture.

Broccoli. Some prefer it raw, as crudités. Either way, as the ancient Romans knew, it's a very healthy member of the cabbage family. Broccoli is the result of deliberate breeding in the northern Mediterranean around 500 BCE. The name is the plural of broccolo, "the flowering crest of a cabbage" and the diminutive of brocco, a small nail or sprout. Broccoli was brought to the U.S. by Italian immigrants but didn't become widespread until the 1920s.

Italy produces two percent of the world's broccoli, and is the fifth biggest producer.

Bronzino (1503-1572) was renowned for his often unemotional yet memorable portraits of the rich. The Florentine son of a butcher was born Agnolo di Cosimo—"Bronzino" was perhaps due to his hair color. He apprenticed with and stayed close to Pontormo, idolized the likewise gay but aloof Michelangelo, and his favorite pupil was Alessandro Allori, with whose family Bronzino was living when he died. A founding member of Florence's Accademia delle Arti del Desegno in 1563, Bronzino was a protégé of Cosimo de Medici, whom he once painted nearly nude as Orpheus.

Mythological guise gave Bronzino license to paint male subjects almost nude, including Andrea Doria as Neptune.

He often painted handsome young aristocrats, and did more than one iconic "Portrait of a Young Man." He also captured the haughty Eleanora of Toledo, among other female subjects.

Bronzino's poems contain proof of his sexuality, as do those of Michelangelo, whose relatives posthumously tried to replace his romantic male pronouns with female ones.

Bruschetta was originally humble peasant fare: a slice of grilled Italian bread rubbed with garlic and drizzled with olive oil (the name is from bruscare, to toast). Then urbanites and non-Italians discovered it, and it became a chic bread choice, often embellished with a variety of ingredients—in Rome it's the in thing with roasted cherry tomatoes (sugar added during the final 30 minutes of the tomatoes' slow cooking caramelizes them to a tempting crispness).

Bulgari the jewelry empire was founded in 1884 by Greek Sotirios Voulgaris (1857-1932), who moved to Rome and became Sotirio Bulgari. (The company spells its name with a Latin or Roman *u* that looks like a modern *v*.) Bulgari's bold and memorable necklace, bracelet, and earring designs drew a rich and famous clientele. The product line expanded to include watches, accessories, fragrances, and cosmetics. Sotirio's two sons took over the business, and during World War II son Costantino and his wife Laura hid three Jewish women in their home in Rome.

Bulgari, which employs some 4,000 people, has over 30 boutiques around the world. The biggest is its ten-story outlet on Tokyo's Ginza.

Cabiria (1914) was hailed by many at the time, and for years to come, as the greatest moving picture yet made. Italy led the world in movie epics during the early silent era—when global audiences weren't divided by languages. After all, Italy had so much history to depict on screen. *Cabiria*, directed by Giovanni Pastrone and written by poet-novelist Gabriele d'Annunzio, was shot in a Turin studio and in Sicily, Tunisia, and the Alps. Its chaste title heroine is a Roman who must deal, passively, with Rome's rival Carthaginians, who are vanquished by fadeout. *Cabiria*'s set pieces include the eruption of Mount Etna, the setting of Roman ships on fire with mirrors, and Hannibal crossing the Alps (elephants and all).

The sets are spectacular and even if the story is often mythical and propagandistic, Pastrone pioneered the use of a dolly and crane for shooting panoramic scenes, slow tracking shots, artificial lighting, and combining background takes filmed on location with studio takes. These innovations greatly impressed and influenced such early U.S. filmmakers as D.W. Griffith and Cecil B. DeMille.

Caesar's Salad was invented ca. 1924 by Caesar Cardini (1896-1956) at his restaurant in the Hotel Caesar on Tijuana's main street, now called Avenida Revolucion. Cesare (original name) had immigrated to California, where he ran a restaurant in Sacramento, the capital, before moving south to San Diego. He was also in business across the border, where there was no Prohibition to contend with. Two of his brothers were restaurateurs in Mexico City.

Caesar's salad became popular with weekenders from Hollywood who visited Mexico to legally drink alcohol, eat, gamble, and relax. The admittedly theatrical Cardini may have introduced the custom of table-side preparation and tossing of the salad by the chef. His salad, whose popularity spread to the north before going international, comprises romaine lettuce dressed with olive oil, lemon juice, Worcestershire sauce, parmesan cheese, egg, garlic, black pepper, and croutons. In 1948 Cardini trademarked his salad dressing.

Cafetiere. The French coffee press uses a plunger to push coffee grounds to the bottom before the coffee is poured. The coffee press often found in stores today was patented in 1929 by Attilio Calimani who furthered the design by using a glass jar with a spout and a close-fitting plunger with a filter on the end. In 1958 Faliero Bondanini received a patent for an improved version of the cafetiere that didn't lose heat so quickly, via an insulated coffee press.

Caffe Florian and Caffe Quadri are Venetian landmarks, opposite each other on St. Mark's Square. Longtime tourist magnets named after their original owners, they serve coffee but also meals, liquor, and liqueurs. Their live orchestras play atmospheric music. Caffe Florian opened in 1720. Clients included Casanova, Goethe, Lord Byron, Henry James, and Proust. Caffe Quadri opened in 1775.

Among its clients: Byron, Balzac, Stendhal, and Richard Wagner, who feared he would someday drown but died in Venice.

Calzone, like so many gems of Italian cuisine, started in Naples. The name means pant leg or stocking. It resembles a folded-over pizza and may have begun as one. It's a filled oven bread made of salted bread dough, inside which are many ingredients typically found on pizzas, including cheeses and sausage meats. Smaller calzones are sometimes fried in olive oil.

In the U.S. traditional calzone dough is made of flour, yeast, olive oil, water, and salt, and non-traditional fillings range from meatballs in chipotle sauce to raspberries and chocolate for dessert calzones. There are even cheeseburger calzones.

Campione d'Italia. Talk about unique geographical oddities. This Italian town, a part of Italy, is inside and entirely surrounded by Switzerland. Which doesn't try to swallow it up. (In the eighth century the town belonged to a man named Totone Campione. Campione's name was extended in the 1930s by Mussolini to Campione d'Italia.)

Switzerland has four official languages: German, French, Italian, and Romansh. The latter, spoken by few, is a Rhaeto-Romanic language, derived from Latin. Rhaetia was a Roman province in the Alps.

Canaletto is synonymous with his hometown of Venice, which he painted so often and so lovingly. Born Giovanni Antonio Canal (1697-1768), his father was also a painter, so junior was nicknamed Canaletto, little Canal, and joined the Guild of Painters in 1720. Chances are if one's seen classic paintings featuring the water and buildings of Venice, at least some are Canaletto's work, or copies of it. Their beauty aside, they serve as records of how that unique city looked in the eighteenth century. Canaletto's work was especially popular in England, to which he moved in 1746, painting English city scenes and landscapes that, however, didn't match the artistry of his work in Venice.

Cannoli is the plural of cannolo, little tube, and they hail from Sicily (most Italians call them cannoli siciliani). Originally a Carnevale treat, their popularity promoted them to year-round status. The tubular shells of fried pastry dough housing a sweet, smooth filling typically containing ricotta cheese range in size from fist-big—especially in Palermo—to finger-sized (cannulicchi).

American cannoli are often filled with mascarpone cream cheese or custard sauce, and may contain chocolate bits, chopped pistachios, candied citrus peel, or cherries at the open ends. Due to their shape, cannoli are sometimes theorized to have begun as fertility symbols. *Chi sa?* Never mind. Food, comfort, enjoy.

Antonio Canova's best-known sculpture is the topless reclining marble statue of Napoleon's sister Paolina Borghese, which rests in Rome's Villa Borghese Gallery. His most famous lost statue was of George Washington for North Carolina's state capital in Raleigh, destroyed during the Civil War. Born near Treviso, Canova (1757-1822) was so talented he could open his own studio in Venice at age 17. Pope Clement XIV helped launch him big-time by giving Antonio the commission for his tomb in 1782. Canova's subsequent output includes a naked bronze statue of Napoleon in Milan and one in London, and an equestrian monument for Charles III in front of the Royal Palace of Naples.

Cantaloupe. There are two species of melon: watermelon and muskmelon. The latter includes the breakfast melons, among them the cantaloupe, small and round, with ribbed skin and orange flesh. Though it possibly originated in Armenia, its first known cultivation was in a papal garden near Rome at Cantaluppi—also called Cantalupo.

Cappuccino now means an espresso—served in a big cup, unlike regular espresso—to which steamed milk has been added. If the milk is properly steamed, rich thick foam materializes atop the coffee. It's become an international favorite in recent decades but in Italy is usually drunk in the morning and rarely after a meal.

The Italian word, from cappuccio—a hood or cowl—derived from cappa—a cape—may also refer to a Capuchin friar (a member of a strict branch of the Franciscan order that wear hoods or cowls) or a South American capuchin monkey, which bears a cowl-like cap of hair on its cute little head.

Capri. The fabled island, not far from Naples or Sorrento, was a favored retreat of Roman emperors Augustus and his stepson Tiberius. During the Renaissance, pirates and plagues reduced Capri's population, but in 1816 an Italian fisherman or a German (sources vary) discovered the Blue Grotto, and the tourist business—now an industry—began in earnest. Artists and celebrities were drawn to visit or live in Capri, which also became a gay mecca for British, German, and Scandinavian notables.

Caravaggio was, like da Vinci, nicknamed after his place of birth. Born Michelangelo Merisi (1571-1610), he was nonconformist and sometimes self-destructive. The leading painter of his day, he was a master of light and shadow—chiaroscuro—and used ordinary people as models, which scandalized many…painters' models were supposed to be highborn. Caravaggio handled oil paints brilliantly and employed unusual points of view and foreshortening to increase his paintings' dramatic tension.

In 1606 he fatally stabbed a tennis opponent and fled Rome to evade police. In 1608 he was jailed in Malta after a violent altercation. He escaped. In 1610 he sailed to Rome in hopes of a papal pardon for the 1606 murder, but when his ship stopped en route he was mistaken for someone else and arrested. Two days later he was released but the ship was gone, along with his possessions. Caravaggio decided to walk to Rome despite the summer heat. He became ill and died. His influence lived on in the art of Velazquez, Murillo, Rembrandt, and Rubens, among others.

Derek Jarman's 1986 *Caravaggio* is a memorable if at times uncomfortable film.

Claudia Cardinale became an international star as the waif-like Indian princess who owns the diamond called *The Pink Panther* (1963). Few of her subsequent films were as widely seen or worthy of her husky-voiced vivacity. Born in Tunisia in 1938, the beauty came too late to Hollywood, which had lost interest in Continental stars. Cardinale acted more than once for Visconti, teamed with semi-plastic stars like Tony Curtis and Rock Hudson, paired sexily with Brigitte Bardot, participated in Werner Herzog's near-legendary *Fitzcarraldo*, was directed by Sergio Leone in *Once Upon a Time in the West*, and returned in *Son of the Pink Panther* (1993, the ninth in the series), starring Roberto Benigni, but she appeared in too many movies in which her roles were inconsequential or repetitive.

Cards. One of the oldest decks of cards was the Visconti-Sforza tarot deck from 1463. Known as trionfi (triumphs, or trumps), they were used for everyday card playing and according to historian Paula Hardy "had a significant impact on the visual composition, card numbering, and interpretation of modern decks."

Steve Carell. Like Will Ferrell, his costar in *Anchorman* (and its inevitable sequel), Carell was a late bloomer by way of TV. The actor-comedian-writer-producer-director spent five years on Jon Stewart's *The Daily Show*, then starred in the U.S. version of *The Office* before cracking movie stardom as *The 40-Year-Old Virgin* in 2005. Carell's vehicles range from funny to goofy to silly and include *Get Smart*, *Despicable Me* (and sequel), *The Way Way Back*, and *Alexander and the Terrible, Horrible, No Good, Very Bad Day*. Carell went memorably serious in *Foxcatcher*.

Born in 1962, the star labeled his company Carousel Productions because "Carousel is derived from my ancestral family name Caroselli," which Steve's father chose to anglicize.

Carnevale. Italy was the birthplace of this "modern" Christian celebration, partly based on the Romans' Saturnalia (via Saturn, god of agriculture and the harvest) and Bacchanalia (via Bacchus, god of viniculture and wine) celebrations. The word, like "carnival," derives from Latin *carn-* (meat) and *levare* (to put away), since meat is prohibited during Lent. Carnevale comes between January 6 and Fat Tuesday (Mardi Gras in French), the day before Ash Wednesday, which marks the start of the fasting days of Lent.

From Italy, Carnevale spread to Spain, Portugal, and France; from France to Germany and New Orleans; and from Spain and Portugal to Latin America.

For a long time, Venice held the most famous and elaborate Carnevale. Today the best are considered to be those in Milan, Lecco, Bellinzona, and Verona, the latter led by King Gnoco.

Carpaccio, an hors d'oeuvre of raw meat or fish, thinly sliced or pounded thin and lightly dressed with assorted condiments, was devised at Harry's Bar by owner Giuseppe Cipriani in 1950 when a good customer, the Contessa Amalia Mocenigo, advised him her doctor had put her on a diet that excluded cooked meat. Cipriani named his creation after Vittore Carpaccio, a sixteenth-century painter noted for his use of reds and whites mirrored in the dish—his work was on display in Venice at the time.

Carrara. The city of Carrara in northern Tuscany is famous for its quarries of high-quality white or blue-grey marble, used for sculpture and building décor since Roman times.

Similar but lower-grade marbles, for example from Turkey, sometimes try to pass themselves off as Carrara and even use the name. In the late 1800s Carrara was "the cradle of anarchism in Italy," partly because the work was so hard and conditions so bad that workers became highly disgruntled. Ex-cons as well as escapees from injustice could apply for work in the quarries, no questions asked. Revolutionaries expelled from Belgium and Switzerland migrated to Carrara, where in 1885 Italy's first anarchist group was founded, leading to the Lunigiana revolt in 1894.

Enrico Caruso retains the title of the greatest tenor ever. Born in 1873 in Naples into a poor family with 18 children, eldest child Enrico worked at menial jobs beginning as a pre-teen to help support his tribe. He made his musical debut in 1895 and became a lead singer in 1900, at La Scala. A singing sensation around the world, he was earning $7,000 a month in pre-taxes-1901. Two years later he debuted at the Metropolitan in New York, where in 1906 he was arrested in Central Park for pinching a woman's bottom and fined a then-substantial $10.

The secret of a great singer's success, he noted, was "Big chest, a big mouth, 90% memory, 10% intelligence, lots of hard work, and something in the heart!"

While singing in Brooklyn in 1920, he began spitting up blood. Several surgeries ensued, but back in Italy he failed to recover from pleurisy and pneumonia and died in 1921.

Giacomo Casanova (1725-1798) has few rivals for the title of history's most famous lover. Born in Venice, he was legally impelled to leave that city due to his love affairs, passing state secrets, and for being a Freemason. Traveling throughout Europe, he lived as a con man—often cheating at gambling—and gained entrée to the best homes and palaces as a distinguished guest and sometimes a lover, encountering VIPs like Catherine the Great, Maria Theresa, Frederick the Great, Louis XIV, George III, and Mozart.

Casanova, who spent time as a librarian in Bohemia, where he died and became famous via the multivolume memoirs that shared his adventures and misadventures, his celebrity socializing, and his 120 love affairs. Several movies have been made of his life, perhaps the best known being Fellini's version.

Luisa Casati was the fashionista precursor to Italian American Lady Gaga and her infamous meat dress and Italian style-star Anna dello Russo with her *Star Wars*-style feathered headgear. The Marquesa Casati (1881-1957), a wealthy heiress by age 15 and thus able to afford her passion for appearances, declared, "I want to be a living work of art." She dyed her hair fire-red, adopted lustrous velvet clothing, and dilated her green eyes with poisonous belladonna ("beautiful lady"). Luisa was painted, sculpted, and photographed by, among others, Cecil Beaton, Dali, Boldoni, Singer Sargent, Epstein, and Man Ray. Buried wearing her false eyelashes, she is remembered as one of the first modern style icons.

Adriana Caselotti was the sweet voice of Snow White in Disney's breakthrough 1937 animated film. Adriana's immigrant father Guido was a music teacher, her mother Maria a singer, and older sister Louise gave voice lessons to Maria Callas in 1946 and '47. Briefly in the chorus at MGM, Caselotti (1916-1997) was signed up in 1935 by Walt Disney, who paid her $970 for her work on *Snow White*. To not spoil "the illusion" of his first movie hit, he prevented her appearing or using her voice in other media or venues, so that her post-*Snow White* career was nearly nil. After Disney's death, Adriana Caselotti sold autographs and made occasional *Snow White*-related appearances.

The Palace of Caserta is known as "the Versailles of Italy." Fifteen miles north of Naples, it was aptly commissioned in 1751 by a great-grandson of Louis XIV—Charles III, King of Naples and Sicily, who also intended a new capital city at Caserta, to be connected with Naples by a broad ceremonial avenue. The city wasn't built, but the 1,200-room palace boasts Italy's most impressive monumental staircase, and the gardens run for miles, punctuated by fountains and fed by a 20-mile aqueduct.

Caserta's architect was Luigi Vanvitelli, the son of Dutch painter Gaspar van Wittel, who'd settled in Rome and Italianized his father's surname.

Cassata, a rich cake once associated with Easter, used to be made exclusively by nuns. Sometimes known as cassata siciliana, it may be as simple as ice cream cake filled with nuts and crystallized fruit or it may be a brick-shaped, liqueur-soaked sponge cake filled with creamed and sweetened ricotta, candied fruits or candied squash and chocolate, then topped and sided with marzipan. Occasionally it's made with layered vanilla, chocolate, strawberry, and pistachio ice cream (cassata ice cream is multi-colored and -flavored, sometimes with fruit and chocolate).

Food writer Mary Taylor Simeti described it this way: "a proper cassata is spectacularly decorative: the cake, striped with marzipan coloured pale green in memory of the days when one could afford to use pistachio paste, is glazed with white icing, and then crystallized wedges of oranges and pears are placed on top, spread out like the petals of a flower within curving ribbons of translucent squash."

Giovanni Domenico Cassini discovered four satellites of Saturn, the second-biggest planet, and recorded the division of its rings—the Cassini Division was named after him, as was the 1997 Cassini spaceprobe that was the fourth to visit Saturn and the first to orbit the giant planet. Cassini

(1625-1712) was a mathematician, astronomer, engineer, and astrologer. In 1669 he moved to France via a grant from Louis XIV to help set up the Paris Observatory, which opened in 1671. Cassini remained its director until his death.

Cassini's method of ascertaining longitude was used to measure the size of France correctly for the first time. (It turned out to be smaller than expected.) Cassini went blind the year before he died.

Oleg Cassini is credited with inventing "the Jackie look" for First Lady Jacqueline Kennedy but also dressed Joan Crawford, Rita Hayworth, Betty Grable, Marilyn Monroe, Gina Lollobrigida, Kim Basinger, and Renee Zellweger. Like his brother Igor, Oleg (1913-2006) used the birth name of his mother Marguerite—the father's surname was Loiewski—who'd founded a fashion house in Florence. Oleg began as a fashion designer in Rome and competed for the Italian Junior Davis Cup and won. In 1936 he moved to the U.S. and soon found work at Paramount Studios. He married actress Gene Tierney and later dated and was engaged to Grace Kelly.

The association with Jackie Kennedy—he designed her A-line sheath and empire strapless dresses—made Cassini (whose brother was a society columnist) a celebrity. Eventually he licensed his name for luggage, cars, nail polish, etc., guested on hundreds of TV talk shows, and did books like *A Thousand Days of Magic—Dressing Jacqueline Kennedy for the White House*. Critics claimed he took too much credit for Jackie's fashion image, but Oleg's personal motto was "Better than most, second to none."

Casting. At first glance, Hollywood casting often seems irrational. Sal(vatore) Mineo read the novel *Midnight Cowboy*, then sought to play Ratso Rizzo in the projected film. But the role (and an Oscar nomination) went to Dustin Hoffman. Robert Blake (*né* Gubitosi) sought to play Santino "Sonny" Corleone in *The Godfather* but the role went to James Caan. The lead role in the movie *Nine*, inspired by Federico Fellini, went to Daniel Day-Lewis—the stage versions had starred Hispanics Raul Julia and Antonio Banderas. On the other hand, when Madonna planned a biopic of Mexican artist Frida Kahlo, the resultant protests dissuaded her and the role (and an Oscar nomination) went to Mexican Salma Hayek.

Benvenuto Cellini resisted his father's wish that he become a musician. A sculptor, Cellini (1500-1571) is best known as a goldsmith—Michelangelo called him "the greatest goldsmith of whom the world has ever heard"—and the author of a racy, self-promoting *Autobiography* that includes assorted and alleged murders. Not published until 1728, the book has never gone out of print. Cellini's most famous sculptures are his *Perseus with the Head of Medusa* (in Florence) and the salt-and-pepper cellar he crafted for French King Francis I (now in Vienna).

In the 1966 movie *How to Steal a Million*, Audrey Hepburn and Peter O'Toole conspire to abduct the fictional "Cellini Venus" from a Paris museum.

Chianti is an internationally popular dry red wine produced in Tuscany and named after the Chianti hills. Chianti Classico must originate in specific parts of the Tuscan provinces of Florence and Siena. Chianti comes from a wider geographic area. To insure quality, Chianti Classico is regulated as to the type and amount of grapes used, alcohol content, and yield per acre, as well as strictly defined borders. The basic grape variety in all Chianti is Sangiovese, which may range from 80 to 100 percent.

Chocolate processing. Until 1728, when English and Dutch smugglers successfully challenged it, Spain monopolized the world's chocolate supply after conquering Mexico in the 1520s. When cocoa beans were introduced to Europe, the Church deemed them dangerous stimulants. The beans reached Italy in 1557 when Piedmont's Duke of Savoy sided with Spain against France and won the battle of St. Quentin. Chocolate processing soon after became a big business in Turin.

As in Mexico, chocolate was a drink in Europe, only becoming a solid after the Dutch alkalized it and released its cocoa-butter content. In the mid 1800s Turin led the way in manufacturing chocolate confections called diablotins (little devils) and givu (cigar tip). Once hazelnuts were added, chocolate candies and bars became more popular than ever.

Christina of Sweden was the most famous northern European to move to Italy—not just for the climate. A monarch in her own right, Christina (1626-1689) refused her advisors' ongoing insistence that she marry. In 1654 she abdicated, relinquishing throne and country for personal freedom.

Christina, praised for being "Italian by choice," was triumphantly received into Rome—and moved into the Farnese Palace. Although or because she was a convert from Protestantism to Catholicism, she advocated the then-radical policy of religious tolerance and worked against anti-Semitism. Christina is buried in St. Peter's Basilica.

Christina II. The ex-ruler wasn't idle in Rome. In 1656 she founded the Accademia dell'Arcadia (Arcadian Academy), dedicated to the pursuit of music, literature, drama, and science. In 1670 she commissioned renowned architect Carlo Fontana to build Rome's first public opera house, the Teatro Tor di Nona. Her second Roman home, the Riario Palace, became a cultural and intellectual center housing a splendid art and book collection—the latter now part of the Vatican Library. Christina wrote books, including biographies of Alexander the Great and Julius Caesar. She was a music patron, among others of Alessandro Scarlatti and Arcangelo

Corelli, and she studied astronomy and mathematics with Giovanni Domenico Cassini—after whom the spaceprobe is named.

Chrysler, long the United States' #3 automaker, is 100 percent Italian-owned since 2014 (FIAT assumed majority control in 2011). Today, Europe's second-largest automaker sells a dozen brands: Abarth, Alfa Romeo, Chrysler, Dodge, Ferrari, FIAT, FIAT Professional, Jeep, Lancia, Maserati, Ram Trucks, and SRT.

Ironically, it was Italian American Lee Iacocca—born in Allentown, PA—who in the 1980s helped save Chrysler from bankruptcy and reversed its fortunes. Chrysler was then able to take over the fourth-place U.S. car manufacturer, American Motors, plus Jeep.

Ciabatta. In the early 1980s a baker in Adria, Veneto, named Arnaldo Cavallari became concerned that imported French baguettes for sandwiches were hurting local bakers. So in 1982 he created ciabatta, "slipper bread," a white bread of wheat flour, water, salt, olive oil, and yeast ideal for sandwiches. The broad, flat bread with a somewhat porous interior has many variations, including crispness of crust, all delicious. By 1999 Cavallari had licensed the recipe to bakers in 11 nations.

Cialde. British food historian Gillian Riley states, "Claims that the ice cream cone was 'invented' in the United States in 1904 are flying in the face of history, for cialde have been around for longer than ice cream." These rolled or cone-shaped cookies or wafers, usually produced between hinged heated plates and sometimes decorated, have served as containers for rich creams and custards for centuries, at least.

Ciao is easy to pronounce (chow) and cool because it means both hello and goodbye—like aloha—without being an oxymoron. In much of Spanish-speaking Latin America, ciao has become part of the language, considered more chic than the local equivalent.

Madonna Louise Veronica Ciccone was born in Bay City, Michigan, in 1958. The bleached-blonde pop princess burst onto the music and video scene in the early '80s and implanted herself in the public eye via publicity that often outraged those who weren't about to buy her product anyway. Though she gave the word Madonna a new spin, she was and remains one of the most influential, dynamic, and chameleon-like pop singers of modern times.

A canny and manipulative businesswoman successful in most showbiz venues apart from motion pictures, Madonna's personal net worth exceeds $500 million. Analyzing herself, she's asserted, "I'm tough, ambitious, and I know exactly what I want. If that makes me a bitch, okay."

Cinecitta (Cinema City) opened in 1937, built on the outskirts of Rome by order of Mussolini, who stated, "Il cinema e l'arma piu forte" (Film is the strongest weapon). Though censorship ruled and creativity was limited, several future leading movie directors trained there, and after WWII—partly due to Hollywood going on location in the 1950s and '60s—Cinecitta became the most famous studio outside the U.S. Said Federico Fellini, who once worked as a cartoonist, "It is like a circus there. With too many clowns. Very colorful…yet somehow good movies get made there."

Cinzano, named after a town in the Piedmont region, is a vermouth available in four versions—Cinzano Rosso (red), Cinzano Bianco (white), Cinzano Extra Dry, and Cinzano Rose (French pronunciation). The product came out of the Turin herbal shop of brothers Giovanni Giacomo and Carlo Stefano Cinzano in 1757. Their "vermouth rosso" incorporated aromatic plants from the Italian Alps in a still-secret recipe combining 35 ingredients, among them thyme, marjoram, and yarrow. Casanova was a fan of the drink, then known as "vermouth of Turin."

Exports began in the 1890s to Argentina, Brazil, and the U.S. In 1912 in Paris, Cinzano was the first product to be advertised with a neon sign. The business remained in the family until 1985.

Giuseppe Cipriani converted a dilapidated monastery on the Giudecca island into Venice's deluxe Cipriani Hotel, going strong since 1958 and including the renowned Ristorante Fortuny—meal prices upward of $100 a person. Cipriani also opened Harry's Bar, near St. Mark's Square, now the anchor to an international brand that includes foods, kitchenware, restaurants, books, and Cinzano. Cipriani once said, "Like the Americans, I believe that making money can be fun."

Rosemary Clooney's first hit song was the Armenian-flavored "Come On-a My House" (1951). Her varied repertoire included catchy Italian-style hits like "Botch-A-Me" (1952) and "Mambo Italiano" (1954). The former was originally "Ba-Ba-Baciami, Piccina" (1941)—baciami means kiss me. Clooney's English version spent 17 weeks on *Billboard* magazine's charts and reached #2. "Mambo Italiano," also recorded by Dean Martin, his daughter Deana, Bette Midler, and others, was via a non-Italian composer and reached #10 in the U.S. and #1 in the U.K. A 1956 Hong Kong version's Chinese lyrics extolled several kinds of Chinese steamed buns.

"The words are sometimes silly, but I love the Italian beat…that Italian sound," said Clooney (aunt to George, who lives in Italy). "Even their language is musical." Pre-stardom, Rosemary sang with Tony Pastor's big band (he was born Anthony Pestritto).

Colosseum is the nickname of Rome's Flavian Amphitheatre, the world's largest, able to accommodate 50,000 to 80,000 spectators. It was begun in the year 70 CE by the emperor Vespasian, patriarch of the Flavian dynasty, and completed in 80 by his son, the emperor Titus. Its inaugural ceremonies lasted 100 days.

The site was most famous for its brutal gladiatorial contests, which lasted until at least 435 CE, when they were last recorded.

The concrete and stone building's nickname may owe to its size or to a huge statue of the hugely egotistical emperor

Nero that stood nearby—the Colossus of Nero, eventually destroyed by angry Romans.

Cole Porter's classic song "You're the Top" begins with "You're the top, you're the Colosseum." Today it's a ruin that still impresses—and somehow manages to look modern.

Christopher Columbus wasn't the first seafarer from the Eastern Hemisphere to discover the Western Hemisphere's Americas—and of course he never landed in what is now the USA—but he made it news and received the credit. Cristoforo Colombo had both vision and persistence. The major seafaring nations at the time were Spain and Portugal, but the redheaded Italian nabbed the assignment and got the job done. Interesting that in English we call him not by his Italian name but by its Latin version.

Too, Italy didn't colonize the Americas and start killing off its native peoples. That was left to Spain, Portugal, France, and England.

Commedia dell'arte is a form of theatre that began in Italy in the 1500s and had a major influence on the stage (including Shakespeare), opera, puppet shows, pantomime, mime, and sketch comedy. It featured stock characters, sometimes masked—a tradition dating back to ancient Greece—enacted by traveling troupes unbeholden to a given theatre or town, except perhaps during Carnevale. Troupes were thus able to employ actresses, and to improvise, which let them satirize local scandals and current events. Instead of costly and cumbersome scenery, they used props, including a baton or stick to mock-beat or -slap an opponent with, ergo a slapstick.

Commedia dell'arte often presented vicarious rebellion—servants against masters, young lovers against restrictive parents, and sometimes wives against husbands, as with Punch and Judy. He evolved from Punchinello (first seen in Britain in 1662), the anglicized form of Pulcinella, a trickster character. Other characters included Arlecchino, later known as Harlequin, a clever servant dressed in a diamond-checked costume and black mask, Scaramuccia, the rogue clown known in Britain and France as Scaramouche, Arlecchino's girlfriend Colombina, aka Columbine, and the stock lovers whose French/English names were Pierrot and Pierette.

Concrete was so well and fully utilized by the Romans, it's often thought they invented it, and for all the improvements they made to it, in a way they did. Theirs was basically a hydraulic-setting cement with similarities to Portland cement, but as Robert Courland wrote in his riveting *Concrete Planet*, Roman cement (with no steel rebar) has far outlasted modern cement, which doesn't endure beyond a few centuries. Despite two millennia of earthquakes throughout the Mediterranean, the buildings, aqueducts, bridges, and other structures built by Rome still stand.

A prime example of Roman engineering: the port of Caesarea, named after Augustus Caesar, in modern-day Israel. Its harbor, built in the first century CE, was the largest artificial harbor yet built in the open sea, constructed using underwater Roman cement technology on a still-awesome scale.

Italia Conti Academy of Theatre Arts. This training school for performers between ages ten and nineteen on London's Great Portland Street was founded in 1911 by actress Italia Conti (1873-1946), known for her way with juvenile actors. It offers a three-year course, and its success may be judged by some of its graduates: Noel Coward, Tracey Ullman, Gertrude Lawrence, Peter Byrne, Anthony Newley, Olivia Hussey, Naomi Campbell, Freddie Bartholomew, Patsy Kensit, and Lena Zavaroni.

Francis Ford Coppola (born 1939) is most closely associated with the *Godfather* film trilogy. An influential director, he's also an Oscar award–winning writer and producer.

Coppola's father Carmine, a flautist and composer, won an Academy Award, and filmmaker daughter Sofia won a writing Oscar. Nephew Nicholas Cage won an acting Oscar, and Francis's sister is actress Talia Shire (*Rocky*), who is also the mother of actor Jason Schwartzman. Coppola's Academy Awards total six, plus he owns a winery. His family originated in Bernalda, Basilicata. As for "Ford," Francis was born in Detroit in the Henry Ford Hospital.

Franco Corelli was in his day an operatic superstar. The handsome lyric tenor (1921-2003) labeled himself "the greatest tenor in the world" and had the professional engagements, the following, and the income to believe it. Clocking in at six feet with an athletic build and wavy black hair, he also believed himself immune to criticism and had a vengeful temper. For instance, in 1958, convinced that bass Boris Christoff was attempting to upstage him, he initiated a real duel onstage that was fortunately non-fatal, if slightly bloody. Corelli was also known to leap off the stage and chase a given heckler around the theatre until other patrons intervened. The word divo applies.

Don Costa (*né* Dominick in 1925) was a music arranger, record producer, guitarist, and conductor. In his teens he joined the CBS Radio Orchestra. His first big break was writing vocal backgrounds for Steve Lawrence and Eydie Gourmé. Another boost was Sinatra hiring him to arrange his 1962 album *Sinatra and Strings*, and he later conducted for Sinatra in Las Vegas. Several of Costa's own instrumental recordings became hits, e.g., "Never On Sunday," which sold over a million copies.

Don and 10-year-old daughter Nikka (*née* Domenica) Costa had an early '80s hit with "Out Here On My Own" and planned a follow-up, but Costa died of a heart attack in 1983. Nikka Costa has continued singing.

Lou Costello (1906-1959) was the shorter, chunkier, and much funnier half—who took 60 percent of their income—of the hugely successful comic duo Abbott and Costello. Louis Cristillo, whose father hailed from Calabria, changed his surname to the Irish Costello (stress on the final syllable). A movie stuntman before teaming with William "Bud" Abbott (1895-1974), Lou's hit movies with Bud helped carry Universal through the 1940s. The boys were a hit on TV too, but personal friction—Lou had tried to change their billing to Costello and Abbott—finally broke them up in 1957.

Lou's final words were reportedly, "That was the best ice cream soda I ever ate."

Cremona is synonymous with violins, especially the Stradivarius created by Antonio Stradivari (1644-1737). His sons carried on the tradition. Two other great violin-making families who began in Cremona are the Amati and Guarneri. The town has two violin-related museums and about 100 violin-making shops. Every third year Cremona hosts an international stringed-instrument expo (the next in 2018). Wealthy and independent, Cremona became a *comune* (city-state) in the eleventh century but was later annexed by the Duchy of Milan.

Crostini means little crusts. The word is sometimes interchangeable with bruschetta. But crostini typically have more complex toppings, from cheese spreads to cooked vegetables to liver pate. Still, the key ingredient for crostini and bruschetta is the bread, which should be chewy, crusty, and firm enough so the topping doesn't cave it in. The toasted bread may be browned on the surface but the inside of the slice ought to remain soft and not dry out as it would in an electric toaster.

Billy Curtis was a handsome, self-confident midget actor 4'2" (1.27 meters) tall, born Luigi Curto (1909-1988) in Springfield, Massachusetts. He starred in the only all-midget western, *The Terror of Tiny Town*, in 1938 and appeared uncredited as a city father in *The Wizard of Oz* the following year. He did numerous TV shows, including *Here's Lucy*, *Gunsmoke*, and *Laverne & Shirley*, and continued acting in films like *High Plains Drifter* and *Little Cigars* (both 1973), the latter about a group of "little people" on a crime spree.

"If I'd been regular-size," he once offered, "I'd have been a big star. The problem with being short is they give us very little dialogue, or none—mostly we're there to be looked at." He also explained that midgets, unlike dwarves, are correctly proportioned.

Martino da Como, sometimes known as Martino di Milano—before what we consider proper last names—was born around 1430 in Torre, then in the Duchy of Milan, now in Switzerland. Little is known about the Western world's first celebrity chef, but ca. 1465 he wrote *Libro de Arte*

Coquinaria (Book of the Art of Cooking), which remained influential for centuries. Its recipes and rules for kitchen etiquette record the transition from medieval to Renaissance cooking. Known as "the prince of cooks," da Como spent much of his career in Rome. One employer was a Cardinal Patriarch known for his sumptuous banquets and prodigal receptions.

An English translation edited by Luigi Ballerini with 50 modernized recipes was published as *The Art of Cooking: The First Modern Cookery Book* in 2005 by the University of California Press.

Giovanni da Verrazzano. New York City's Verrazano-Narrows Bridge connects Brooklyn with Staten Island and opened in 1964. It's named after this intrepid explorer (ca. 1485-1528) born near Chianti, Tuscany—the family castle still stands. In France he entered the service of Francis I and sailed to Canada in 1508. In 1524 he failed to find a northwest passage to East Asia but in 1525 reached the Carolinas, and then headed north, discovering New York Bay and Cape Cod before turning back for home at Newfoundland.

Da Verrazzano's 1528 voyage was his last, to the Caribbean. After landing in what was likely Guadeloupe, his rowboat was impeded by rocks, so he jumped out and swam ashore, solo. He was captured by the man-eating Caribs, killed, and consumed, within sight of his helpless brother and crew.

Joe Dallesandro, born Joseph Angelo D'Allesandro III in Pensacola in 1948, had a harsh upbringing. His non-Italian mother was in jail for interstate auto theft. Joe survived foster homes (his younger brother later took his life), street gangs, and run-ins with the law thanks to modeling and acting. He became the biggest of Andy Warhol's Factory-made "superstars" and the leading male sex symbol of underground American film. In the 1960s and '70s he starred in such cult movies as *Trash*, *Heat*, *Flesh*, and *Lonesome Cowboys*. He also worked in Europe and had small roles in mainstream films.

Now semi-retired, he reportedly manages a Los Angeles apartment building.

Dante Alighieri (1265-1321) is often called by just his first name. Outside Italy he is best known for *The Divine Comedy*, a three-part literary visit to hell, purgatory, and heaven. In Italy, Dante is the national poet, revered—except by extreme regionalists—for helping develop the Tuscan dialect into a national language to replace Latin. In 1302 Dante's nationalist sympathies got him expelled from his native Florence. He also criticized the corruption of the Church.

At the time of his death at 56 from malaria, Dante was living in Ravenna. As his posthumous fame grew, Florence requested—in 1396, 1429, and 1476—that his bones be returned. Ravenna always refused. When a Florentine pope threatened to take the remains by force, they were hidden away for almost 150 years. Dante's bones remain in Ravenna, and his so-called tomb (built in 1829) in a Florence church is a hollow memorial.

> **Dante in D.C.** L'altissimo poeta, as he's known in Italian, is honored at least thrice in Washington, D.C. The Library of Congress has a marble bust of him. The Italian Cultural Center, or Casa Italiana, boasts a full-size marble statue. Largest is an outsized bronze statue from a model by Italian Ettore Ximenes (1855-1926), who did sculptural work on Rome's "Wedding Cake" monument. This impressive memorial was put up at Meridian Hill Park in 1921, the 600th anniversary of Dante's death, by immigrant Carlo Barsotti, a newspaper magnate. The 12-acre park, purchased by the U.S. government after the Civil War, was considered for a while as the possible site of a new White House.

Bobby Darin (1936-1973), born Walden Robert Cassotto, grew up thinking his mother Nina was his sister and that his grandmother was his mother. The deception, practiced until 1968, was due to the stigma placed upon unwed mothers. Because of rheumatic fever, Bobby wasn't expected to live much beyond age 20. In his teens he already played several musical instruments, then became a songwriter for

Connie Francis before penning his own million-seller, "Splish Splash," in 1958. Other hits included "Dream Lover," "Mack the Knife, and "Beyond the Sea".

Darin, a recording and nightclub star, also succeeded in movies, earning a supporting Oscar nomination as a shell-shocked soldier in *Captain Newman, M.D*. He married Sandra Dee, his costar in *Come September*, which top-billed Rock Hudson and Gina Lollobrigida. Increasingly politically active, Bobby was present at the Ambassador Hotel the night presidential candidate Robert F. Kennedy was assassinated in 1968. Darin's true parentage was disclosed to him partly in case he ran for political office. He died at 37.

> Bobby's maternal grandmother Polly—whom he'd believed was his mother—had been a vaudeville singer. Repeating that music was "in your blood," she promoted his interest in musical instruments, singing, and songwriting. Darin's maternal grandfather, Saverio Antonio "Big Sam Curly" Cassotto, was a would-be mafia kingpin who died of pneumonia in prison a year before Bobby's birth in the Bronx.

David, by Donatello, was the first freestanding male-nude statue created since antiquity as well as the first unsupported standing work of bronze cast during the Renaissance. David wears a laurel-topped hat and boots, one foot posed atop Goliath's head, as he holds the slain giant's sword. Now in Florence's Museo Nazionale del Bargello and executed ca. 1430 or the 1440s (sources vary), this playful, almost child-like David contrasts with Michelangelo's more mature, more intense David.

David, by Michelangelo, is one of the most famous statues in the world, reproduced countless times in myriad contexts—e.g., atop a fountain in Mexico City's Plaza Rio de Janeiro or the ice sculpture that features hilariously in the 1997 movie *My Best Friend's Wedding*. The original, carved of Carrara marble between 1501 and 1504, stands 17 feet (5.18 meters) tall in Florence's Accademia di Belle Arte. Until 1873 it stood al fresco in the Piazza della Signoria, where a copy now stands—another Florentine copy is at the Piazzale Michelangelo. His David, with its power and solemn beauty representing the triumph of justice over brute force, made Michelangelo, 29, the leading sculptor of his day.

Originally intended for Florence's cathedral, David was so admired that it was set up in front of the city hall.

David di Donatello Award is Italy's equivalent of Hollywood's Academy Award and is named after Donatello's statue of David. The award is a mini version in gold on a malachite base with a gold plaque citing the category (there are 24), year, and winner. The awards, begun in 1955 and given by L'Accademia del Cinema Italiano, were organized by journalist and producer Michael Stern (later the founder of The Michael Stern Parkinson's Research Foundation in New York City).

Giorgio De Chirico was born in Greece (1888-1978) of a Genovese mother and Sicilian father. Before World War I he founded the "scuola metafisica" art movement that would greatly impact surrealism. Ironically, De Chirico later moved toward a traditional painting style, though often reproducing metaphysical themes from his earlier work which other artists borrowed from or even semi-appropriated. In the

1970s Andy Warhol opined, "One third to one half of Dali's subjects were stolen from De Chirico. I can't even guess why the Italian didn't sue him." Working in a neoclassical or neo-Baroque style, De Chirico remained prolific into his late eighties.

His writer-painter brother Andrea became famous as Alberto Savinio.

Niccolo De Conti. One of the fifteenth century's more interesting bestsellers was the true story of merchant and voyager Niccolo De Conti (ca. 1395-ca. 1469), born near Venice but off to Damascus as a teenager working as a trader's assistant. Learning local languages along the way, he moved to India in 1414, married an Indian, and had several children but continued traveling for a quarter century, visiting Sri Lanka, Indonesia, Thailand, Burma, and probably China. In 1440 he finally decided to go home, but in Cairo was detained and forced to become a Muslim. Unable to leave, he lost his wife and two children to a plague before managing to escape with his surviving offspring. He finally reached Venice in 1444.

To De Conti's shock, the exaggerated tale of his 30 years' travels was already selling in book form via a Spaniard he'd met in the Middle East. The pope then ordered De Conti to dictate his true story, which was written by noted Florentine humanist Poggio Bracciolini and became a 1400s bestseller.

Robert De Niro (born 1943) got off to a slow start in movies, due to his phlegmatic personality, admitted shyness, and poor cold-reading skills. But he made up for it, with and without directors like Martin Scorsese and Francis Coppola. He won a supporting Oscar as the young Vito Corleone in *The Godfather Part II* (1974) and a Best Actor Oscar for *Raging Bull* (1980) as boxer Jake LaMotta. In his later years, De Niro has demonstrated comic talent in films like *Meet the Parents* and its sequel *Meet the Fockers*.

De Niro's mother Virginia Admiral was a painter and poet. His father was a painter. Son Raphael, reportedly named after the hotel in Rome where he was conceived, is a real estate tycoon in New York City.

Vittorio De Sica (1901-1974) appeared in about 150 movies and was a distinguished if often humorous presence. Outside Italy he was better known as an actor than a master director, although four of his movies won Academy Awards for Best Foreign Language Film. Teaming with screenwriter Cesare Zavattini, the director produced such classics as *Shoeshine*, *The Bicycle Thief*, and *Umberto D*. He also helmed *Two Women*, *The Garden of the Finzi-Continis*, and *Yesterday, Today, and Tomorrow*.

Death in Venice by Thomas Mann has been described as a story about the most beautiful boy in the world set in the most beautiful city in the world. When director Luchino

Visconti made a 1971 movie of the 1912 German novella, he changed the protagonist from a professor to a composer, in keeping with the Italian mood of the platonic love story. Composer Sir Benjamin Britten made an opera of *Death in Venice* in 1973.

For all its beauty and romantic allure, Venice, as Mann made clear, lives on water—not always the healthiest place to be.

Carmen Dell'Orifice. At age 13, she was approached to model, and at 15 she appeared on the cover of *Vogue*. Half Italian and half Hungarian, the New Yorker was pretty but unspectacular until her hair turned prematurely white. In the modeling world she is legendary; born in 1931, she is the oldest working model ever, and still owned the runway during the 2012 spring/summer season. In 2011 Dell'Orifice received an honorary doctorate from the University of the Arts in London in recognition of her contribution to the fashion industry. In 2013 she stated, "I've had more covers in the past 15 years than I had in all the years before that." Svelte and stunning, the 5'10" Carmen has long embodied the glamour of high fashion.

Personally, she had less luck. Husband #1 pocketed her money and put her on a meager allowance. #2 left her after she decided to retire in 1958 (she returned in 1978). #3, a young architect, lasted nine years. Dell'Orifice was engaged to TV producer David Susskind, who died before the marriage. There followed a long-term boyfriend whose best friend was Bernie Madoff, with whom Carmen invested—and then lost—her life savings. But isn't looking fantastic for your age really the best revenge?

Danny DeVito grabbed fame by the throat on TV's hit series *Taxi* (1978-1983) as Louie DePalma, the small (4'11"/1.5 meters) but large-tempered cab dispatcher. Born in New Jersey in 1944, his family was originally from San Fele, Basilicata. Post-TV, DeVito became an unlikely star in movies like *Ruthless People*, *The War of the Roses*, *Hoffa*, and *Batman Returns* (as The Penguin). He also directed major pictures, and his company Jersey Films produced such hits as *Erin Brockovich*, *Pulp Fiction*, and *Get Shorty*. A vegan, Danny is an animal-rights activist.

Leonardo Di Caprio's company is Appian Way Productions. Nonetheless, the actor-producer-environmentalist (born 1974) is but a quarter of Italian origin. His mother is German-born and his father, whose father hailed from near Naples, is German on his mother's side. Only-child Leo, who made his screen bow in 1991, has played Italian in *Romeo and Juliet* (1996) and Italian American in *Catch Me If You Can* (2002), based on real-life con man Frank William Abagnale Jr. who had eight separate identities that included a doctor, a lawyer, a pilot, and a U.S. Bureau of Prisons agent. In 2011 *Catch Me If You Can* became a Broadway musical.

Joe DiMaggio's entire baseball career was spent with the New York Yankees. A three-time Most Valuable Player, he was an All-Star in each of his 13 seasons with the team. In 1939 he was nicknamed the Yankee Clipper—his "speed and range in the outfield" were compared to the then-new Pan American Clipper airliner. Joe's brothers Vince and Dom were also Major League center fielders.

The 1954 marriage of DiMaggio to Marilyn Monroe didn't last out the year but made both that much more famous. (Joe had already been married to an actress by whom he had a son.) After Marilyn, with whom he remained friends, he didn't remarry and never spoke about her in public.

> After Japan's 1941 attack on Pearl Harbor, the U.S. also declared war on Nazi Germany and Fascist Italy. Ergo, Joe DiMaggio's Sicilian immigrant parents Giuseppe and Rosalia were suddenly classified as "enemy aliens." They were required to carry photo-ID booklets at all times and weren't permitted to travel beyond a five-mile radius from their home without permission. Giuseppe was banned from San Francisco Bay, where he'd fished for decades, and his boat was seized. Nonetheless in 1944 Rosalia became a U.S. citizen, as did Giuseppe in 1945.

Dolce and Gabbana. *The New Yorker* observed in 2005 that Milan-based "Dolce and Gabbana are becoming to the 2000s what Prada was to the 1990s and Armani was to the 1980s—gli stilisti (the stylists) whose sensibility defines the decade." The trendy couple's designs ranged from playful (underwear as outerwear) to retro (gangster pinstripe suits) to exhibitionistic (extravagantly printed coats), appealing to more daring and youthful fashionistas.

Domenico Dolce, born in Sicily in 1958, and Stefano Gabbana, born in Venice in 1962, met in 1980, moved in together, went into business, and by 1986 proved they could do high fashion as well as launch an eye-catching empire that embraces clothes, purses, sunglasses, watches, cosmetics, fragrances, etc.—advertised often, boldly, and sometimes controversially.

La dolce far niente. "To be Italian is more about living well than being ambitious," stated actor-director Vittorio De Sica, "but unfortunately the two usually go together." It's been said the true Italian pastime is doing nothing, and la dolce far niente means the sweetness of doing nothing. Writer Gore Vidal, who had two homes in Italy, explained, "How sweet just to sit and watch, then walk in the sun, sit again with an espresso watching people and waiting for a wonderful meal…when in Italy, do as the Italians do."

La Dolce Vita means the sweet or good life. The title of Federico Fellini's 1960 movie wasn't translated into English and became a household phrase internationally. The Marcello Mastroianni starrer—with memorable input from Swedish Anita Ekberg, who moved to Rome—looked at Italian high society in a new way and explored social changes being induced by the media. The Catholic Church tried to have *La Dolce Vita* banned, which resulted in massive free publicity. The film was a hit, a *succes de scandale*, and a *succes d'estime* that made Fellini influential and a media force.

Donatello was his nickname because Donato di Niccolo di Betto Bardi (ca. 1385-1466) was short, although not on talent. Historian Luciano Mangiafico claims he was "arguably, the greatest sculptor of his time. Ghiberti may have been more refined, Michelangelo more powerful, but Donatello's versatility with all types of material—wood, marble, clay, and bronze—and his imaginative, emotional, expressive use of sculpture topped them."

Besides his David in Florence, another Donatello masterpiece is his monument to soldier of fortune Gattamelata in Padua—the first monumental equestrian bronze statue since ancient Rome. Thanks to Donatello's repute and his friendship with Cosimo de Medici, he is buried next to the Florentine ruler in the city's San Lorenzo Church.

Donatello is also the name of one of the Teenage Mutant Ninja Turtles. The other three are Leonardo, Michelangelo, and Raphael.

Aldo Donelli, nicknamed Buff, was born in Naples but moved to the U.S. as a child. In the 1934 World Cup, he scored the only goal for the United States during a 7-1 loss to the host, Italy. After 1934 Donelli played soccer professionally in Italy before returning to the U.S., where he became the only individual coaching pro and college teams simultaneously. In 1941 he coached at Duquesne University, which went undefeated in eight contests. But for part of that season, he was also head coach of the Pittsburgh Steelers, who lost all five games under Donelli's direction. As they say, you can't win 'em all.

Andrea Doria. Those who've heard the name usually associate it with the passenger liner that sank in 1956, costing some 50 lives (sources vary). That ship was named after Italy's greatest naval hero (1466-1560), an admiral from a noble Genovese family who was a condottiero, literally a contractor, who hired out to rulers like Francis I and Charles V for their interminable wars. He also undertook several expeditions against the Ottoman empire's then-dominance of the Mediterranean. In most of his campaigns Doria was successful, in all of them active. At 84, Doria once more put out to sea, against Barbary pirates.

Earlier, having helped expel the French from Genoa, Doria helped rewrite its constitution (which was still pro-aristocrats, but Italian ones). Yet he declined to become Genoa's ruler.

Two U.S. Navy ships were named after Andrea Doria—in 1775 and 1908—also two battleships, one retired in 1929, and the other ironically in 1956. Andrea Doria was also the name of an Italian missile cruiser built in 1964 and decommissioned in 1991.

Eleonora Duse, often known as just Duse or la Duse, was the Meryl Streep of her day (1858-1924), rivaled only by Sarah Bernhardt. Impartial theatre-goers like Irishman George Bernard Shaw usually declared Duse the more natural and talented thespian. Where Bernhardt was outgoing and loved publicity, Duse, born in Vigevano, Lombardy (she died in Pittsburgh), was introverted, loved reading, and shunned interviews, preferring her performances to speak for themselves. Raised in poverty, she began acting at four, the daughter and granddaughter of actors.

An occasional theatrical manager and director, Duse was sometimes kept off-stage for years by ill health. In 1896 she concluded a highly successful U.S. tour in Washington, D.C., where every night's performance was attended by President Grover Cleveland and his wife. The First Lady created a society scandal when she held the first White House tea for an actress. In 1923 la Duse was the first woman and first Italian to grace the cover of *Time* magazine.

Duse and Deledda. The only filmed performance of Eleonora Duse is in the 1916 silent movie *Cenere* (Ashes), from the novel by Sardinian writer Grazia Deledda (1871-1936), the first Italian woman to win the Nobel Prize for Literature, in 1926. Duse co-wrote the screenplay and enacted a mother who sacrifices all for her son. The novel spotlighted poverty, poor health, illegitimacy, illiteracy, and the woes of the lower classes. Duse made no more films, declaring, "I am too old."

Grazia Deledda's first short-story collection was published when she was 19, despite her formal education having been limited to three years of primary school. Her novels were sometimes compared to George Sand's and Chekhov's. Though Deledda wrote often about women oppressed by patriarchal society, she might today be considered a pioneering feminist author and her work would be more widely read if her female characters weren't so uniformly passive.

Eateries in Italy are conveniently named and divided into categories. A ristorante is a restaurant, whether elegant and expensive or simple and traditional. A trattoria is a small, usually family-owned restaurant, cheaper than a ristorante. A rosticceria sells food to go, much of it roasted. There are two kinds of pizzerias: those that sell pizza by the slice and the sit-down types. A paninoteca sells sandwiches, a gelateria sells ice cream, and a pasticceria sells pastries. Some are take-away, some sit-down.

There's an Italian saying: A tavola si sta sempre in allegria—At table one is always happy. It refers basically to one's home table but applies to any Italian table where food is served. Buon appetito!

Eating out in Italy can be somewhat different. For one thing, portions may be half to a third the size of American ones. Yes, there's less obesity in Italy, but a meal there often comprises three or four courses. A salad is usually served after, not before, the entrée—else the dressing's vinegar would clash with the wine consumed during the meal. Salad is meant to cleanse the palate and prepare it for the next course!

Italian restaurants seldom serve butter—their bread is good enough without it—or that Californian creation, the oil-balsamic vinegar dip. Soup and/or salad rarely come with an entrée, except in a menu turistico. Vegetables continue the à la carte tradition and are ordered separately. There's typically a cover charge for the bread, linen, and silverware, and most non-tourist-oriented eateries don't open for dinner until 8 p.m.

Elba, an island of 90 square miles, lies some eight miles off the Tuscan coast and was therefore a foolish choice on which to exile the captured Napoleon, its most famous resident. Elba was colonized over 4,000 years ago for its copper and iron. Its last iron mine was active until 1981. Elba was also renowned for its wine. The Roman writer Pliny the Elder dubbed it "the Island of Good Wine."

In 1814 Napoleon was brought to Elba, where he was given a town house and a country villa—in other words, treated like royalty. He stayed less than ten months, escaping to again become emperor of France and would-be conqueror of Europe. Until he met his Waterloo in 1815. After that, he was exiled to the more remote island of St. Helena in the South Atlantic.

Perhaps the most famous palindrome is the Napoleonic lament "Able was I ere I saw Elba."

Eleonora of Arborea is a Sardinian and feminist heroine. From 1383 to 1404 she was a governing giudicessa— judge—of Arborea, one of the island's four administrative divisions. She opposed foreign rule and exhorted Sardinians to resist Spanish invaders. Also, she completed the codification of laws that her father had begun. Written in Sardinian rather than Latin, they were revolutionary in establishing community property in marriage and allowing women the right of redress in cases of rape.

Ernesto is the title and protagonist of poet Umberto Saba's 1953 autobiographical novel, unfinished and unpublished until 1975 (akin to E.M. Forster's posthumously published *Maurice*, dedicated "To a Happier Year"). Born Umberto Poli (1883-1957) in Trieste, the Jewish Saba's popular poems suppressed his sexual orientation. *Ernesto*, of which he wrote only five chapters, concerns a 16-year-old in 1898 Trieste who has an affair with a 28-year-old laborer (known only as "the man"). Guilt eventually sends Ernesto to a female prostitute. He ends the affair, focuses on his violin, and now 17, meets Emilio, a handsome 15-year-old fellow violinist.

The 1979 movie version directed by Salvatore Samperi took liberties with the story, changing the period to 1911 and marrying Ernesto off at the end to Emilio's twin sister!

Espresso means fast. Italians talk fast, drive fast, etc. Italians don't like to wait around for coffee. Why everything so fast? So they can save enough time to take it easy and enjoy la dolce vita! Therefore the espresso machine that produces Italy's national drink was born of impatience and the need for speed. It's called espresso because the hot water was expressed through the coffee expressly for one customer in an express time. Whether customers wanted their coffee ristretto—more concentrated—or lunghetto—a tad more diluted—or lungo—yet more diluted—each espresso was individually tailored by the machine operator or, more currently, the barista.

> **Espresso glossary.**
> Caffe latte—half espresso, half hot milk, usually drunk in the morning.
> Corretto—espresso "corrected" with a shot of brandy, grappa, or sambuca.
> Decaffeinato—decaffeinated.
> Doppio—a double espresso.
> Lungo—a less concentrated espresso that may fill the demitasse almost to the top.
> Macchiato—espresso with a dash of warm milk (macchiato literally means stained). A lungho macchiato has a bit more water than a regular espresso and is crowned with a dollop of thick milk foam.
> Ristretto—concentrated and strong espresso.

Espresso machines. The first coffee machine to use steam to force hot water through finely ground beans was invented by Frenchman Louis Bernard Rabaut in 1822. But in 1901 Luigi Bezzera created the definitive espresso machine.

In 1903 he sold his patent to Desiderio Pavoni in Milan, who began making and selling espresso machines in 1905, as did Victoria Arduino in Turin. Their sales were restrained by the burnt taste that exposure of the grounds directly to the steam sometimes produced.

Milanese pastry shop owner Achille Gaggia was ever seeking a better coffeemaker and in 1938 bought the patent of a late inventor named Cremonesi for a new machine that forced water through the coffee with a piston. World War II interfered, but in 1948 Gaggia, according to coffee historian Morton Satin, "changed the world of coffee forever with a new machine called the Classica that eliminated direct steam injection. At a temperature of precisely 92 degrees C (197.6 F), water from a small boiler was forced through the coffee at approximately nine atmospheres of pressure by means of a hand pump.

"The result was a revolution: an espresso capped by a head of foamy crema....From that moment on, having a fine crema—that heavenly caramel-colored emulsion of essential coffee oils floating on the surface—has been the goal of all espresso makers."

Et cetera. Yes, it's Latin—which makes it Italian, if not Italian-language. It's such a clever way of expressing what it does, from *et* (and) and *cetera* (the rest), that several languages, including English, use it. It certainly rolls off the tongue easier than the German *zum Beispiel*. And it's so nicely abbreviated: etc. Always feel free to correct those who mispronounce it eck-cetera.

"Et tu, Brute?" Even those who haven't read Shakespeare's *Julius Caesar* know that this (literally: And you, Brutus?) is shorthand for stunned disappointment at betrayal by someone you trusted implicitly.

For the historically challenged, after Julius Caesar made himself Rome's dictator for life he was struck down—stabbed—by a group of more democratically-minded Romans that included his close friend Brutus. Ironically, Caesar's great-nephew Octavian (renamed Augustus) became the first Roman emperor not long after.

Fabian was born Fabiano Anthony Forte in Philadelphia in 1942. His whirlwind musical career—he later called it "frightening…a three-year nightmare"—began with his 1957 discovery by Bob Marcucci and Peter DeAngelis, owners of Chancellor Records. Often mocked for his one name, his pompadour, and his white bucks, Fabian had 11 song hits before buying out his contract with Marcucci for a reported $75,000. During the 1960s payola scandal, Fabian testified before Congress that his voice had been electronically altered to "significantly improve my voice."

Switching to acting, initially in light movie fare, Fabian later earned praise in television drama. From 1969 on, he was billed as Fabian Forte. In 1973 he posed nearly nude in *Playgirl* magazine and later made comebacks on the music-nostalgia concert circuit.

Oriana Fallaci was a tougher international version of Barbara Walters. The feisty Florentine (1929-2006) hailed from a family of rebels and anti-Fascist fighters and fought against "the arrogance of power and the intransigence of fanaticism." Oriana removed the required veil in front of Ayatollah Khomeini, argued with Yasser Arafat, insulted Federico Fellini, got shot during student protests in Mexico, covered the Vietnam War from the battlefields, and got Henry Kissinger to admit that war's futility (he called it "the single most disastrous conversation I have ever had with any member of the press"). After 9/11 she frequently assailed Islamic fundamentalism,

Muslim terrorists, and the increase in Muslim immigration into Europe.

Fallaci became a journalist (like her uncle Bruno Fallaci) in her late teens and published her first book in 1954. In later years she lived and worked in New York, but returned to Florence before losing her lengthy battle against cancer. Upon her death, Italy's president Giorgio Napolitano said, "We have lost a journalist of world fame, an author of great editorial success, a passionate protagonist of lively cultural battles." Pier Ferdinando Casini, ex-speaker of the Italian parliament declared, "Oriana Fallaci was the greatest Italian journalist of the last century."

Farinelli (1705-1782), like a modern-day pop star, was known by one name. He was the most famous castrato of them all, a Neapolitan whose publicity held that his testicles were amputated after a riding accident. However like most castrati his status was more probably due to an impoverished father and/or a music-loving Church elder. After vocal training in Naples and Bologna, Carlo Farinelli debuted in 1720 and stunned audiences with his incomparable "golden voice."

Farinelli's career took him through Europe's leading opera houses, but much of it was spent performing privately for royalty. In 1737 Spain's Queen Isabella contracted him to sing exclusively for her husband Philip V, an insomniac depressive who later went insane. Carlo Farinelli was employed at Philip's court for ten years, then by the next Spanish king. He wasn't as liked by the following king, who fired him with the words, "Capons are only good to eat," whereupon Farinelli finally returned to Italy.

The overlooked (in the U.S.) 1994 film *Farinelli* starring Stefano Dionisi is a visual and aural delight.

Fashionista. The term, coined in 1993, now denotes, per the *Concise Oxford English Dictionary*, a designer of haute couture or a devoted follower of fashion. It first appeared in Stephen Fried's biography of Gia Carangi, referring to the entourage encircling a supermodel at a photo shoot. The word was partly inspired by "Sandinista," the Nicaraguan pro-democracy movement that overthrew dictator Anastasio Somoza. Terms like barista, for a coffee bar employee, follow the same pattern.

Gia Carangi (1960-1986) was a supermodel who besides myriad magazine covers appeared in ads for Armani, Versace, Dior, and Yves Saint Laurent. A heroin addict, she died of AIDS and was portrayed by Angelina Jolie in the TV movie *Gia* in 1998.

Anthony Fauci, immunologist, is the world's leading authority on avian flu and holds over 30 honorary degrees. Born in Brooklyn in 1940 to Italian immigrants, he became a medical doctor at Cornell University in 1966 and went on to head the National Institute of Allergy and Infectious Diseases. He played a key role in discovering how HIV leads to AIDS and is at the forefront of research into a vaccine to prevent HIV infection. Dr. Fauci has written, coauthored, or edited over 1,000 scientific publications, including several textbooks for future doctors.

Federico Fellini's films are memorable less for their plots than their look and, often, the unique, even grotesque faces of the non-actors and actors in them. Chief among his thespic protégés were wife Giulietta Masina (*La Strada*, *Juliet of the Spirits*, *Nights of Cabiria*, the latter adapted into the Broadway musical and movie *Sweet Charity*) and Marcello Mastroianni (*La Dolce Vita*, *8½* — adapted into the Broadway musical and movie *Nine* — *Ginger and Fred*, also with Masina).

Fellini (1920-1993) worked early on with Roberto Rossellini but developed a totally distinctive, recognizable style and by the 1960s could add his name to a movie's title — e.g., *Fellini Satyricon*, *Fellini Roma*, *Fellini Casanova* — to draw spectators and, often, controversy. Four Fellini pictures won Best Foreign-Language Film Oscars.

La Fenice (The Phoenix), Venice's leading opera house, is shockingly well named. In 1792, during construction, it partially burned. In 1836 it burned down. And in 1996 two behind-schedule electricians rewiring La Fenice set fire to it rather than face a $30,000 fine. Again it rose from the ashes and reopened in 2004.

La Fenice was the site of debut performances of Verdi's *Rigoletto* and *La Traviata*, Rossini's *Semiramide*, Stravinsky's *The Rake's Progress*, and others.

In the 1600s opera was so popular in Venice, La Fenice was able to support 16 opera houses.

Enrico Fermi for worse and for better helped usher in the nuclear age. The brilliant Roman graduate of the University of Pisa (founded in 1343) was part of a group conducting experiments on nuclear fission at a physics laboratory in Rome. But in 1938, because Fermi's wife Laura Capon was Jewish, the couple could be persecuted in Italy via Nazi-influenced anti-Semitic laws. So when Fermi traveled to Stockholm to receive the Nobel Prize for Physics, he chose not to return. He and his family moved to New York, where he became a professor at Columbia University. In 1942 Fermi executed the first controlled nuclear chain reaction—the start of the atomic age.

At Los Alamos, New Mexico, Fermi helped construct the atom bomb. After World War II he continued research at the University of Chicago, where he taught. In 1954 he died of stomach cancer at age 53.

Fernet-Branca's smell has been described as "black licorice-flavored Listerine." It's very bitter—also available as sweeter mint-flavored Branca Menta—and is often drunk neat as a *digestif* after a meal, in a cordial glass. It's also a non-primary ingredient in cocktails like the Fanciulli, Toronto, and Hanky Panky. Its North American popularity has risen with increased interest in "vintage" cocktails.

Fernet-Branca was created in Milan in 1845 by Bernardino Branca. Its recipe, a secret to this day, includes saffron, myrrh, cardamom, rhubarb, chamomile, and aloe, with a base of grape distilled spirits, plus caramel coloring. In Italy it may be served room temperature or with ice and is sometimes mixed into one's coffee or espresso.

In Argentina, with its huge Italian community, Fernet-Branca is especially popular and is typically mixed with cola or soda water.

Ferragamo is sometimes labeled the Rolls-Royce of shoes. Naples-born (1898-1960) Salvatore Ferragamo began making and selling shoes from his parents' home in his early teens. In 1914 he immigrated to Boston. Later, with a brother, he moved to Los Angeles, where Sal's stylish and necessarily pricey footwear found favor with Hollywood stars. Repatriated to Italy, Salvatore opened a shop in Florence that went bankrupt by 1933. After the Depression and World War II, the persistent Ferragamo's fortunes improved, and by 1950 he was overseeing 700 artisan shoemakers who daily created 350 pairs of shoes.

Two of Ferragamo's sons eventually ran the business and opened the Museo Salvatore Ferragamo in Florence, a shoe-design museum, in tribute to their father.

Ferrari didn't begin manufacturing street-legal automobiles until 1947. Enzo Ferrari's company, founded in Maranello in 1929, originally sponsored drivers and produced race cars. Speed and endurance were Enzo's focus; he sold road cars in order to fund his Scuderia Ferrari, the firm's original name (scuderia means stable, and the corporate symbol remains a prancing black stallion on a yellow shield). Ferrari was particularly involved with Formula One racing. The company product was deliberately high-speed and high-status.

In 1969 FIAT bought a half interest in the company. In 1988, the year Enzo died, Ferrari debuted its F40, one of the most famous supercars ever. From 2002 to 2004 the company produced their fastest model yet—$650,000 per vehicle—named the Enzo.

The highest price ever paid for an auctioned car was in August, 2014, in Carmel, California, for a 1962 Ferrari 250 GTO Berlinetta: $38.1 million.

Geraldine Ferraro was the first woman to run for U.S. vice president on the ticket of a major party. She was also the first Italian American (born in 1935 in New York State to an Italian

American mother and a father from Campania). Initially a teacher, Ferraro became an attorney who specialized in fighting sex crimes, domestic violence, and child abuse. In 1978 the New York Democrat was elected to Congress, where she sought reforms for women's equity in wages, pensions, and retirement plans. In 1984 former Vice President Walter Mondale chose Ferraro for his running mate.

Ferraro twice ran for the Senate and during the Clinton administration was appointed U.S. ambassador to the United Nations Commission on Human Rights (1993-1996). She continued her work as a journalist, author, and businesswoman, and in 2008 campaigned on behalf of Hillary Rodham Clinton's presidential bid. Geraldine Ferraro died at age 75 in 2011 of multiple myeloma, 12 years after her diagnosis.

Fiasco in English means a big failure, but it's an Italian word meaning bottle, related to the English flask, from the Latin *flasca*. When and how did fiasco become so negative? It happened in the 1800s via the Italian slang "far fiasco" (to make a bottle) which signified failing in a theatrical performance. In Italy today fiasco often refers to a cheaper bottle of Chianti cradled in an atmospheric straw basket.

Fiasco baskets were born of practicality, to protect wine bottles during transportation and handling and to provide a flat base so rounded bottles can have round bottoms—easier to make by glass blowing. The straw is usually sala, a swamp weed dried in the sun and bleached with sulfur. By the early 1900s Italy employed some 1,000 glass blowers and 30,000 basket weavers to make fiasco baskets.

The straw bands may be vertical or horizontal. The base is a donut made of scrap straw tied with fine straw blades. The process has become increasingly automated since the 1950s.

FIAT. The acronym stands for Fabbrica Italiana Automobili Torino. The company was founded in Turin in 1899 by a group of investors including Giovanni Agnelli, whose grandson Gianni famously led FIAT from 1966 to 1996. Besides an impressive array of practical small cars, FIAT has manufactured farm tractors, railroad engines and carriages, aircraft, and military vehicles.

Over the decades, FIAT acquired smaller Italian automakers and has employed more than 100,000 Italians at a time. The company's international presence is strong; its biggest production site outside Italy is Brazil, where FIAT is the #1 automobile.

After several lackluster years, FIAT is riding high again— and now also owns Chrysler. Notta bad, eh?

Fibonacci. (1170-ca. 1250) The neglected-in-his-lifetime mathematician went by just Leonardo, was sometimes called Leonardo Pisano after his hometown of Pisa, and was nicknamed Fibonacci since he was a figlio, or son, of the Bonacci family. The Fibonacci numbers or Fibonacci sequence, part of his work in numbers theory and ignored during the Middle Ages, are his legacy. Briefly, the first two numbers in the Fibonacci sequence are 1 and 1 or 0 and 1, depending on the chosen starting point, and each subsequent number is the sum of the previous two.

The sequence appeared independently in Indian metaphysics, relating to Sanskrit prosody. Such sequences are also found in nature, e.g., branching in trees, the arrangement of leaves on a stem, the flowering of an artichoke, and the family tree of honeybees. Leonardo was fond of mathematical equations, riddles, and puzzles. Perhaps his most famous went "A certain man put a pair of rabbits in a place surrounded by a wall. How many pairs of rabbits can be produced from that pair in a year if it is supposed that every month each pair begets a new pair which from the second month on becomes productive?"

Leonardo wrote several textbooks but lived before the printing press, so each book and every copy had to be handwritten, and several of his original books have not survived.

The Fibonacci Quarterly is a journal entirely about the study of Fibonacci numbers.

Flora. The first book ever written about plants for their own sake, for ornamental rather than medicinal purposes, was *Flora, o Vero Cultura dei Fiori* (*Flora, or True Flower Culture*) by Giovanni Battista Ferrari, published in 1638 and influential for centuries to come. It provided a myriad of tips and advice on everything from the ideal garden guard dog to the alteration of flower color, form, and scent.

Flora was the Roman goddess of flowers and spring.

Florence—Firenze, that is—is the city most intimately tied to the Renaissance, thanks to Leonardo da Vinci, Michelangelo, Botticelli, and an army of great artists, but also leaders cum patrons of the arts like Cosimo de Medici and his grandson Lorenzo the Magnificent. Florence is one of the world's richest treasure troves, bursting with art and history. Nature and excellent food are also close at hand, with the

Ponte Vecchio over the Arno River, the Boboli Gardens, the best of Tuscan cuisine, superior Chianti in cafés galore, and gelato so delicious people argue passionately whether it's better in Rome or Florence. There are also nearby picturesque villages, beautiful towns, and historic cities that usually each merit an individual stay or return visit.

A Florentine is a native of Florence but a florentine is a delicious, rather artistic cookie with chopped or diced nuts and sometimes preserved fruit, chocolate-coated on one side.

Florentine is a more inviting way of indicating that a food includes spinach. Being Italian, it's no chore to eat and you needn't close your eyes and envision Popeye's muscles to get it down. Eggs Florentine are practically as good as Eggs Benedict, and few would consider cannelloni or manicotti—tubular rolls of pasta whose stuffing sometimes includes spinach—health food…just delicious food.

The association of Florence with spinach is due to native daughter Catherine de Medici (1519-1589), who when she moved to France in 1533 to marry the dauphin took along her own Italian cooks and spinach seeds. She had her cooks prepare several dishes featuring spinach, which the French court called à la Florentine. Catherine may or may not have been paranoid, but she feared poison and became a less than popular non-French queen, like the later Marie Antoinette.

Focaccia. The ancient Romans had *panis focacius*, a flat bread baked on the hearth. Its name came from *focus*, Latin for hearth or place of baking. In recent decades the rest of the world has discovered flat, oven-baked focaccia, typically made from high-gluten flour, oil, water, salt, and yeast—it's usually punctured to avoid bubbling on top—and baked in a stone-bottom or hearth oven. Focaccia is often crowned with herbs or flavored with vegetables and kept moist with a smearing of olive oil. In Italy it may accompany a meal or be covered with cheese, onions, and meat, or used as a pizza base or for sandwiches (the latter is its most common North American use).

Foreign fruits, vegetables, flowers, etc. Histories of the Renaissance sometimes overlook the influence upon thought, philosophy, curiosity, self-image, art, décor, botany, medicine, and certainly cuisine of the importation to Europe of previously unknown fruits, vegetables, flowers, herbs, and spices from the Americas and Asia. For instance tomatoes and maize from Mexico, potatoes from Peru, eggplant from India, and tulips from Persia and Turkey, not to mention spices that were often literally worth their weight in gold.

Fork comes from *furca*, Latin for pitchfork. Surprisingly, forks were little used in northern Europe until the 1700s and in the U.S. until the 1800s. Ancient Egyptians used them as cooking utensils, but not at the table. Table forks appear to have reached southern Europe via the Byzantine Empire. In 1533 forks reached France when Italy's Catherine de Medici wed the future King Henri II. But the French were slow to accept forks, deeming them an affectation. More religious types called them "unnatural"—competition for God-given fingers.

In 1608 Englishman Thomas Coryate brought the first forks to England after using them in Italy. In the 1400s forks had begun turning up in Italian cookbooks.

In eighteenth-century America a spoon was usually held in the left hand to steady meat as it was cut with the right hand's knife before the spoon switched to the right hand to shovel the morsel into the mouth. By the Civil War, forks had become unobjectionable.

Formaggio di Fossa. Fossa means hole, pit, or grave, and if the idea of burying a cow's or sheep's milk cheese in a ditch for three months seems odd, consider China's so-called 100-year-old eggs. Food historian Gillian Riley notes the resultant aroma is "rich in the pungent whiff of woodland undergrowth...the flavour is delicate, almost mild, at first, with a piquant and increasingly bitter aftertaste."

The ditches are actually pits—in northern Italy, particularly Emilia-Romagna—carved out of the tufo or volcanic rock, purified by fire, lined with fresh straw and reeds, sealed with layers of wooden planks and sand, with each prepared cheese wrapped in clean white cloths with the name of the owner. Underground fermentation also augments the cheese's nutritional qualities and makes it easier to digest.

The Fountain of Trevi, named after Rome's Trevi district, is possibly the world's most famous fountain. Tradition holds that if one tosses a coin backwards into it, one is guaranteed a return to Rome. Some 3,000 euros' worth of coins land in the fountain daily, the proceeds supporting a supermarket for Rome's poor. The fountain's location is the end point of an ancient aqueduct. In the early Renaissance a fountain was built there, then restored in the 1600s. The current Baroque fountain, by Nicola Salvi, was completed in 1762. It features Neptune astride a winged chariot led by two tritons (mermen). Its side niches harbor statues of Health and Abundance, while four other statues represent the seasons.

The fountain, 86 feet high, gushes 17.5 million recycled gallons of water a day. It was memorably filmed in Fellini's 1960 classic *La Dolce Vita*, also *Three Coins in the Fountain* (1954), in which only two coins were tossed in! The title song, with music by Jule Styne and lyrics by Sammy Cahn, won that year's Best Song Academy Award.

Connie Francis was the world's top-selling female singer in the late 1950s and early '60s. Born Concetta Rosa Maria Franconero in 1938 in Newark, her throbbing, emotional delivery made hits of "Who's Sorry Now," "Among My Souvenirs," "Don't Break the Heart That Loves You," etc., and "Where the Boys Are," from her 1960 debut movie of the same name. Other hits included "Al Di La," "Volare," and "Tango Italiano." The success of her 1959 album *Connie Francis Sings Italian Favorites* led to her recording in several languages and expanding her international popularity.

In 2009 Connie was given a star on the Italian Walk of Fame in Toronto.

Francis I of France was an unabashed Italophile who seemed impervious to French art and artists. He commissioned goldsmith Benvenuto Cellini to create tableware and sculpture for him and requested friendly Italian leaders to send him paintings by Tiziano and Bronzino. Francois (1494-1547) imported Italian artists to design and decorate his palaces outside Paris, the Chateau de Madrid and Fontainebleau (later famous as the home of Napoleon). Some French artists at court soon adopted aspects of Italian painting, the better to suit the king.

> Francis I's greatest artistic coup was persuading 65-year-old Leonardo da Vinci to leave Italy in 1516 and move to the palace of Cloux, near the king's residence at Amboise, near Tours. Francois bestowed on Leonardo the title "First painter, architect, and mechanic of the king." The genius had few duties and was treated as an honored guest. He died in France in 1519 and that is why the Mona Lisa—La Gioconda—hangs in Paris.

St. Francis of Assisi is associated with birds and animals—he preached to them as he did to people—and with poverty and humility. He was born in 1181 or '82 while his father, a prosperous silk merchant, was away. His mother named him Giovanni after John the Baptist. When his father returned, he renamed him Francesco, "the Frenchman," after his French customers. Uninterested in business, young Francesco Bernardone reportedly led a dissolute life.

When war broke out between Assisi and Perugia, he was captured and jailed for a year prior to his ransom. Francesco, who was never ordained a priest because he felt unworthy, spent more and more time with the sick and poor, and in prayer. He alienated his father by giving away what he could of his father's property. Eventually Francesco renounced his patrimony and took a vow of absolute poverty. He composed his still-popular "Canticle of Brother Sun" poem and set it to music. Francesco, who died in 1226 and was canonized in 1228, is considered the founder of all Franciscan orders and is credited with bringing a more charitable outlook and practice to the medieval Church.

Friday. In the Latin languages, Friday is named after Venus, the goddess of love and beauty (Rome's version of Greece's Aphrodite). The Latin for Venus was Veneris. In Italian, Friday is Venerdì, in French *Vendredi*, in Spanish *Viernes*, etc. Interesting that the adjective for Venus, venereal, has only a negative connotation in English. "Friday" is named after Frigg, the Olde English love-goddess equivalent.

Frittata is a flat Italian omelet that's often served at room temperature and may be cut into wedges. Its base is egg and precooked vegetables like mushrooms, zucchini, asparagus, or artichokes, and sometimes cheese, ham, or bacon. Any number of pastas may also be incorporated, multiplying the frittata's variations. Rolled frittatas have been around for centuries, as seen in the work of painter Pontormo (1494-1557).

"Funiculi, Funicula." Most everyone's heard this 1880 song, whether in the original Neapolitan or English or standard Italian or instrumentally. But few outside Italy would guess it was written—music by Luigi Denza, lyrics by Peppino Turco—to commemorate the opening of the first funicular cable car on Mt. Vesuvius (destroyed by the volcano's eruption in 1944). The title means "funicular up, funicular down," and the song has been recorded by everyone from Mario Lanza and Connie Francis to Luciano Pavarotti and Alvin and the Chipmunks.

The Futurist Cookbook by Filippo Marinetti (1876-1944), published in 1932, was no bestseller. Most people considered it nonsense, and some were enraged by its suggestions, such as avoiding pasta or placing certain foods on the table solely for one's visual and olfactory enjoyment. Marinetti believed food is more than fuel for the body, that it's an esthetic experience and can affect how one thinks, acts, and dreams. He advocated contrasts in flavor, color, and texture, and emphasized vegetables' nutritional value. Though he had his quirks, Marinetti was in some ways ahead of his time.

The Galata Tower, built by Italians in the mid-fourteenth century, soars 219 feet (67 meters) in easternmost Europe, in Istanbul, just west of the Bosphorus, which separates Europe and Asia. The tower attests to the far-reaching economic and military power of northern Italy's city-states in the Middle Ages. Galata, the walled city north of the Golden Horn—the waterway dividing north and south in the European part of Constantinople—was a prosperous Genoese colony that didn't immediately fall to the invading Ottoman Turks in 1453. The cone-topped tower was the apex of the outpost's impressive fortifications, which the sultan in the 1800s approved tearing down. British, Italian, and other diplomats protested, and the Galata Tower, at least, was saved. Today a major tourist attraction, the Romanesque tower's elevator ascends to an unremarkable restaurant and to an unforgettable 360-degree view of two continents and the former capital of two empires, the Byzantine and the Ottoman.

Galileo Galilei (1564-1642). Around 100 CE cartographer Claudius Ptolemy devised the Ptolemaic Theory that the universe revolves around the earth. This was accepted by virtually all astronomers and endorsed by the Church but not Galileo. At age 25 a full professor of mathematics at the University of Pisa, he began postulating laws of motion and acceleration. Increasingly interested in astronomy, he built a telescope that could magnify objects thirtyfold. His discoveries included the four moons of Jupiter (named after the chief Roman god), that Venus circumambulates the sun, and that the sun itself rotates.

After Galileo wrote in a letter that the Bible couldn't always be taken literally and became vocal about his conviction that the earth rotates around the sun, he was tried by the Holy Inquisition and found guilty of heresy. Though he recanted to save his life, his books were thenceforth banned from print. Galileo died deaf and almost blind at 78.

> Why is Galileo Galilei usually known only by his first name and nearly never by just his last name (unlike, say, Garbo)? Because Galilei was not his surname; rather, it's a variation of the one name his father's family had used for generations. (Likewise, the painter Arcimboldo was sometimes called Arcimboldi.) At the time Gaileo was born, in 1564, surnames were optional in Italy. During his lifetime several city-states passed laws requiring last and first names to be officially registered.

Vincenzo Galileo and Chu Tsai-Yu. During the 1500s mathematicians attempted to solve the problem of producing a musical scale that worked properly for all the combinations of 12 notes. Vincenzo Galilei (father of Galileo) came up with the solution in 1581, as did Chinese scholar Chu Tsai-Yü a year before him—of course neither knew of the other. Both men were waved off and their correct answers ignored for a century or so—the equal temperament system didn't come into general use until the late 1700s. Essentially, musicians felt that mathematicians should mind their own numerical business. The British piano makers Broadwood proudly refused to change to the new, better system until 1846.

Galleria Vittorio Emanuele II, directly across from Milan's Duomo, is a soaring, majestic iron-and-glass neoclassical arcade opened in 1877 that represented the new Italy's potential and pioneered the concept of a luxurious covered shopping and eating complex. Still nicknamed "Milan's living room," its influence is seen in countless megamalls the world over.

Tragically, architect Giuseppe Mengoni plummeted to his death from the scaffolding just before the king inaugurated the arcade.

Galliano is a sweet herbal liqueur with a vanilla-anise flavor created in 1896 by brandy maker Arturo Vaccari of Livorno. It was named for Giuseppe Galliano, a hero of the First Italo-Ethiopian War (1895-1896) that basically pitted empire-hungry Italy against French- and Russian-backed Ethiopia. The bitingly yellow color symbolizes the gold rushes of the 1890s and the bottle shape reprises a classical Roman column. Among Galliano's ingredients are vanilla, star anise, Mediterranean anise, ginger, citrus, juniper, musk yarrow, and lavender.

Galliano is both a "digestivo" and an ingredient in cocktails like the Golden Dream, Golden Cadillac, and Harvey Wallbanger.

> The Galliano Company produces other internationally popular liqueurs, including a white Sambuca, a black Sambuca, and an amaretto. They also make Galliano Ristretto coffee-flavored liqueur and Galliano Balsamico, a balsamic vinegar–infused liqueur. Galliano liqueur itself has acquired new popularity via a Brooklyn cocktail named Mr. October, which the *New York Times* said "tastes like apple pie à la mode, thanks to Galliano's vanilla notes."

Robert C. Gallo, along with a French doctor, discovered that HIV causes AIDS. Born in 1937 to immigrant parents in Waterbury, Connecticut, Dr. Gallo worked at the National Cancer Institute at the National Institutes of Health in Bethesda, Maryland, from 1966 to 1996. Gallo, who furthermore discovered the virus that causes leukemia, also developed the AIDS blood test. He has been awarded 19 honorary degrees.

Luigi Galvani. (1737-1798) This Bolognese physiologist became famous via his discovery in 1780 of the twitching of frogs' legs in an electric field. It happened when his wife Lucia served them for dinner and Luigi noticed one leg was still twitching. He deduced that this was caused by a latent power he named animal electricity, conducted to the muscles by a fluid. He invented an electrostatic machine to duplicate the effect he'd witnessed. Galvani's name became an adjective—galvanic, involving electric currents produced by chemical action—and a noun—galvanism, electricity produced by chemical action or the therapeutic use of electric currents. And the verb to galvanize is to shock or excite something or someone into action.

Galvani's nephew Giovanni Aldini was more gruesomely minded. In 1802 in London he publicly demonstrated the application of electric current to nerves in the bodies of executed criminals, which produced facial contortions and spontaneous muscular contractions. Many therefore believed galvanism might restore the dead to life, a belief that may have inspired Mary Shelley to write her 1818 novel about executed-criminal body parts being electrically brought to life by a scientist named Frankenstein.

Giuseppe Garibaldi (1807-1882) is the figure most closely associated with Italy's unification. One of a triumvirate, he was sometimes labeled the sword of independence, while Giuseppe Mazzini was its intellectual firebrand and Count Camillo Benso of Cavour its wily politician-diplomat. Garibaldi is known as "the Hero of the Two Worlds" because he also fought in France and for the independence of the province of Rio Grande do Sul from Brazil (unsuccessfully) and of Uruguay (successfully). In the early 1850s, Garibaldi, who had to flee Italy, lived in Staten Island, New York, where his home is now a museum.

Garibaldi eventually became an admiral, a general in seven countries, and a member of parliament in five countries. President Lincoln offered him the position of major general in the Union Armies. Garibaldi's most celebrated exploit was sailing to Sicily with a small army that managed to overthrow the much larger one of the corrupt local kingdom, thus adding the southern island to the kingdom of Italy.

Gelato. Italian ice cream is often described as the world's best. It's made with less cream than milk—so, with less fat content one can better taste its fruits, nuts, or other flavoring ingredients. Gelato melts more readily on the tongue and seems fresher and lighter than other ice creams. It may use eggs and is traditionally minus the chemicals and stabilizers of mass-produced brands and so needs to be eaten soon after production, usually within 24 hours.

> A few variations of gelato are "cream" ice cream, lemon ice cream, cinnamon ice cream, Ricotta ice cream, and Mascarpone ice cream, the latter two incorporating dessert cheeses. Cassata is a mixture of ice cream and candied fruit. Semifreddo (semi-cold) is a mixture of ice cream, cake, and fruit.
>
> Italy's best ice creams are usually locally made. A vendor's sign may say Produzione Propria (made by the proprietor), ergo fresher ice cream than more commercial versions.

Gestures (i gesti) are an intrinsic part of speech in Italy. Italians are known for using their hands, which help indicate the depth of expression. Many or most gestures are easily understood, however the gesture for bye-bye or ciao resembles the Anglo come-here and that for enough or basta approximates calling a safe in baseball. Plus there are at least half a dozen gestures for, uh, get stuffed. Naturally, gestures may vary in different parts of the country.

Lorenzo Ghiberti. Talk about dedication—or a one-track though celebrated career. The artist (1378-1455) spent most of his adult life creating two sets of doors for the baptistery of Florence's cathedral. His first commission, in 1401 (to commemorate the city's surviving the plague), was won against Brunelleschi, who subsequently turned to architecture. Ghiberti began casting the bronze doors two years later and finished them in 1424; his apprentices included Donatello and others who later became painters. Cathedral authorities were so pleased with the results that they gave Ghiberti a commission for a second set of doors, on which he labored from 1425 to 1452. Their admirer Michelangelo dubbed them "the gates of paradise," which they've been called ever since.

Riccardo Giacconi won the Nobel Prize for Physics in 2002 for discovering the sources of cosmic X-rays. Born in Genoa in 1931, he got his Ph.D. in physics from the University of Milan in 1954, then moved to the U.S. two years later, specializing in experimental astrophysics. He taught and did research at several universities, including Princeton, MIT, Harvard, and Johns Hopkins. Additionally, he was the first director of the Hubble Space Telescope Institute.

A.P. Giannini (1870-1949) founded what was for a long time the biggest bank in the world. The son of immigrants from the Genoa area, Amadeo Peter Giannini was born in San Jose, California. He never went to college and became involved in the produce business with his stepfather until, through his wife, he became director of a small immigrant bank in San Francisco. In 1904 he opened his own Bank of Italy, which prospered after the city's earthquake-induced great fire of 1906 by honoring his commitments and loaning money to help rebuild San Francisco. By 1930 the bank had changed names to the Bank of America and by 1946 was the world's largest private bank.

Giorgione, tall or big George, is the *nom d'art* of Giorgio Barbarelli da Castelfranco, born in Castefranco, Veneto, in 1477 or '78. One of the greatest yet most enigmatic of Renaissance painters, almost nothing is known about his personal life. He did apprentice under Giovanni Bellini, the leading Venetian master of his day, and in the early 1500s was so closely imitated by Titian, Palma Vecchio, Lorenzo Lotto, and others that it's often difficult to differentiate their works.

Giorgione, who died at 32 or 33, probably of the plague, was perhaps the first Italian to paint landscapes with people in them for their own sake rather than for religious or historical purposes. They were meant as movable works in their own frames. His colors were especially intense and glowing. His best known efforts are the *Sleeping Venus*, a prototype for Titian's *Venus of Urbino* and many reclining female nudes to come, and his portrait of a "Youth," an idealization of the

Renaissance male whose chiseled effect seems to overlap from painting into sculpture.

Il Giornale could be considered the forerunner of Starbucks. The brainchild of Howard Schultz, it was inspired by his 1983 trip to Italy that included a prolonged visit to a Milano espresso bar where he witnessed all manner of coffee being served in a friendly, comfortable atmosphere. Other coffee bars, whether small and cozy or large and elegant, convinced him the concept could succeed in the U.S., where Schultz had taken over marketing for Starbucks the year before. The chain comprised five stores that sold coffee but not beverages.

Starbucks' three owners didn't want to go into the coffee bar business, but Schultz persuaded them to give it a try, and in 1984 the sixth Starbucks became the first to sell beverages and was an instant success. The owners still resisted the new direction, so in 1985 Schultz quit and opened Il Giornale, meaning The Daily, which even included background opera music. He soon had three shops in Seattle and Vancouver. In 1987 the owners of Starbucks chose to sell, and Schultz bought them out, becoming the president and CEO of the future megachain, whose concept has been described as "a comforting blend of a retail coffee store and an Italian-type espresso bar."

Schultz, born in Brooklyn's subsidized Bayview Projects in 1952, is now worth over $2.2 billion.

Gnocchi may be translated as dumplings but are much more. They can be made with or without flour, from potatoes, corn meal, or bread crumbs. They may contain herbs, cheese, vegetables or sweeteners like cocoa or prunes! Spinach gnocchi are just one variation. Gnocchi are typically cooked in lots of salted water, then bathed in a given sauce—some gnocchi have a textured surface (usually grooved), the better to hold sauce—or just melted butter or cheese. Gnocchi may be served as a first course to a meat entrée or as a side dish. Either way, delish!

King Gnoco, named after a dumpling, leads the colorful Carnevale of Verona. The tradition dates back to the early 1500s, when the town experienced a serious famine that reportedly was relieved by those who could afford dumplings giving them to the starving poor. It's nice to think those harsh times weren't entirely, uh, Machiavellian.

Gnoco is Venetian for the standard gnocco.

Gorgonzola is Italy's blue cheese, naturally fermented from cow's milk. Its greenish-blue marbleizing originated in the eleventh century, and the cheese is named after a town near

Milan in the Po river valley. Gorgonzola may be buttery or firm. A two- to three-month-old Gorgonzola has a mild, sweet taste and creamy texture, while a mature one aged five to six months has a pungent flavor. Either may conclude a meal, accompanying pears or grapes, or can be used in pasta and risotto sauces.

Under Italian law the cheese enjoys Protected Geographical Status as to its provenance.

The Grand Tour was a long-established tradition for Brits and Americans who could afford to travel the continent at leisure, often for a few months or more, to get "an education," albeit an informal one (and sometimes a sexual one, for males). It endowed the traveler with status and cachet when one returned home. The tour usually took in France and perhaps a corner of Germany and a Low Country or two but invariably included and typically focused on Italy. Period-film director James Ivory explained, "Italy was the cradle… of art and romance and beauty. Also, its people were much closer to their classic past than those of Greece."

English novelist Barbara Cartland observed, "A young person of quality's upbringing and education were capped by doing the Grand Tour. Exploring a goodly handful of Italian cities was a required cultural and social credential."

Granita goes back long before snow cones. In the sixteenth and seventeenth centuries, Italian doctors battled each other recommending or denouncing chilled drinks. Grainy and sweetened, granitas lend themselves to a myriad of flavors. A favorite is Lemon Granita, simply made with water and sugar boiled into a syrup, lemon zest, and lemon juice, the combination later broken into ice crystals that harden to make a slush which pours into small glasses.

Another favorite is Granita di Caffe con Panna, comprising crystals of strong sweet coffee generously overlaid with unsweetened whipped cream.

Grappa is a spirit made chiefly and cheaply in northern Italy from the compressed grape seeds, skins, stems, and pulp that remain after the juice has been pressed out for wine. It's one part pomace to one part water, distilled in a copper cauldron. Traditional grappa is a strong, even harsh "firewater," but recent decades have seen higher-quality grappa produced from better grapes.

Gucci began in 1921 as a saddler and leather-goods store in Florence, via Guccio Gucci, who in 1938 opened the House of Gucci's flagship store in Rome on the fashionable Via Condotti. The company diversified into deluxe scarves, ties, shoes, purses, and more. Boosting the international status of Gucci and its double-G insignia was a bamboo handbag worn by Ingrid Bergman in the 1954 Roberto Rossellini film *Viaggio in Italia*. Eldest son Aldo ran the Gucci Empire from 1953 to 1986 but was eventually sentenced to U.S. prison for tax evasion. In 1987 Gucci was sold to investors. Today there are nearly 300 Gucci stores worldwide.

A Gucci competitor is the **Pucci** Empire founded by the ignoble Emilio Pucci, born a marquis in 1914 and a member of Italy's Olympic ski team in 1934. He took up fashion as a hobby in 1935, designing ski clothes. In the '50s he branched into casual wear, scarves, bags, shoes, and lingerie. In the late '60s he became a member of Italy's parliament—as a member of the neo-Fascist party.

To Guido or not to Guido? *Jersey Shore*, MTV's controversial top-rated reality show, was often accused of showcasing Italian American stereotypes. Comedian Lisa Lampanelli said, "Any show focusing on one ethnic group is going to be labeled tacky and cliché. The question is, how fun is it? I got tired of watching those Guidettes put up with those jackass Guidos—like the one on season two who tried to throw his girlfriend's mattress out the second-floor window, with her still on it!"

When the show went on location to Florence, Italy, many locals cold-shouldered the cast, feeling *Jersey Shore* cast all Italians in a negative, more-typical-of-southern-Italians mold. One Florentine columnist asked, "What if anything is 'Italian' about these vulgar young Americans who cannot speak Italian?"

The more low-key *Everybody Loves Raymond* also had its detractors. Doris Roberts, who played mama Marie Barone, offered, "Most people who watched it enjoyed it, but I tell you, some very vocal people of Italian ancestry would let me hear their displeasure with Raymond's *famiglia*. I tried to stop them and say, 'Darling, blame the writers, not me. Anyway, I'm Jewish.'"

Harry's Bar in Venice was declared a national landmark in 2001. Opened in 1931 by Giuseppe Cipriani, it became famous for the famous people who frequented it, not to mention its Bellini cocktail and carpaccio hors d'oeuvres. Harry's was also the place to drink and be seen drinking a very dry martini. The name Harry came either from a rich young Bostonian acquaintance or Giuseppe's son Arrigo.

History. For about 1,500 years, from the fall of Rome's empire to the late 1800s, Italy—that is, its city states—was the coveted object of its mightier neighbors' greed and their rulers' ambitions. Spain, Austria, and France continually competed for pieces of the peninsula. Much of that time, Spain owned half the country, letting the South stagnate in poverty, illiteracy, and benighted religiosity (e.g., the Holy Inquisition terrorizing southern Italy longer than elsewhere, and the castration of boys to make them Church singers after it was illegal in the North).

As history professor Joseph F. Pritivera put it, "It was a long period during which Italy was defenseless and helpless, under the control of powerful foreign nations. That it had created modern civilization for Europe availed it not at all." Pritivera admitted that the country had been despoiled too by its own "voracious feudal lords, yet could produce one of the richest cultures—with some of the finest architecture, painting, sculpture, and literature—in the world." Italy's contributions (and Dr. Pritivera left out cuisine!) well exceed those of most nations, and match those of the top handful.

I Love Lucy had several episodes that rank among television's funniest ever. One was "Lucy's Italian Movie," in which she learns of an upcoming film titled *Bitter Grapes* (à la *Bitter Rice*, which made Silvana Mangano a star). To prepare for the hoped-for role, Lucy Ricardo goes grape-stomping in a vat occupied by feisty, no-nonsense Teresa Tirelli(1907-1989), who at one point pins her down longer than Lucille Ball expected. "She was strong...she scared me!" Tirelli was reportedly a real-life grape-stomper. After all her trouble and purple-stained skin, Lucy finds out the title is merely symbolic—and Ethel gets the role.

Lee Iacocca, the son of immigrants, was born Lido Anthony Iacocca in 1924. He went to work for Ford as an engineer and helped design such cars as the Mustang, Ford Escort, Lincoln Continental Mark III, Mercury Cougar, and Mercury Marquis. His rise at Ford was eventually stymied by clashes with Henry Ford II, and in 1978 "Lee" was fired—the same year that Ford posted a $2 billion profit.

Iacocca was wooed by a sorely ailing Chrysler, which he proceeded to turn around as its president and CEO, becoming one of the 1980s' most publicized and admired business leaders. He retired from Chrysler in 1992.

Though his parents honeymooned at Venice's Lido, Iacocca has denied his first name derives from that beachy locale.

Ices and Ice cream The ancient Romans made iced wine and fruit juices and knew how to preserve ice in summer. When Catherine de Medici arrived in France to marry the dauphin she brought a Florentine cook aptly named Buontalenti who ushered water ices into the French court (who called them *sorbets*). An Italian named De Mirra apparently introduced water ices to the English court of Charles I. Summertime Italian fruit ices have remained popular in Europe for centuries, e.g., orange ices comprising whole oranges filled with water ice, tasting of the fresh juice.

Ice cream as we know it—milk-based, as opposed to sherbet—was apparently invented by the Chinese. In the late 1700s the famous Italian café owner Tortoni made ice cream using fresh cream instead of water, while Giovanni Bosio of Genoa was probably the first person to sell ice cream in the U.S., in New York in 1770.

The Idolmaker was a 1980 movie *à clef* about singing-star-maker Bob Marcucci, who'd proposed the project and served as technical consultant, and two of his discoveries, allegedly based on Frankie Avalon and Fabian. Written by Edward Di Lorenzo, who also wrote for TV's *Miami Vice*, it depicts the escalating obsessiveness of songwriter/manager Vincent "Vinnie" Vacarri (Ray Sharkey), who first promotes saxophonist Tomaso DeLorusso (Paul Land, *né* Paul Calandrillo) into hit-singer Tommy Dee. The Svengali then does the same for and to a busboy named Guido (Peter Gallagher), who becomes Caesare—one name, like Fabian. (Sharkey won a Golden Globe in the title role.)

Italian American Museum of Los Angeles. This downtown L.A. museum, opened in 2015, illustrates the difference between the Los Angeles Italian experience and that of Italian immigrants elsewhere in the U.S. It reminds that once, prejudice against Italians was widespread and deep. In some parts of the U.S. during the nineteenth century, Italian Catholics were the second-most common targets of lynchings. In the early twentieth century, eugenicists deemed Italians racially inferior and political cartoons depicted Italians as rats incarnating the "ills of immigration." By contrast, in Los Angeles, which began as a Spanish and then a Mexican town, Italians encountered minimal hostility.

For further information, visit www.italianhall.org.

Italian American sports figures—a piccolo sample.

- Yogi Berra, born in 1925, was one of baseball's best catchers, his 19-year playing career spent mostly with the New York Yankees. As a player, coach, or manager, he appeared in 21 World Series and won 13.

- Brian Boitano, figure skater (born in 1963), was a 1988 Olympic champion, 1986 and '88

World Champion, and 1985-88 U.S. National Champion. He came out before the 2014 Winter Olympics in Sochi to protest homophobia in Putin's Russia.

- Jennifer Capriati is a former world champion—rated #1—tennis player born in 1976 who retired in 2004.

- Rocky Graziano, enacted by Paul Newman in *Somebody Up There Likes Me* (1956) and born Thomas Rocco Barbella (1919-1990), was a famed "knockout artist" often able to take out an opponent with a single punch.

- Rocky Marciano, born Rocco Francis Marchegiano (1923-1969), was the sole boxer to hold the heavyweight title and go untied and undefeated throughout his career, successfully defending his title six times.

- Joe Montana (born in 1956) was one of football's best quarterbacks, spending 14 of his 16 playing seasons with the San Francisco 49ers. Nicknamed Joe Cool and a sports sex symbol, he won four Super Bowls and three Super Bowl Most Valuable Player awards.

- Tommy Lasorda, former baseball player born in 1927, enjoyed a long career in sports management, spending some six decades with the Brooklyn/Los Angeles Dodgers.
- Vince Lombardi (1913-1970), football player, coach, and sports executive, was best known as head coach of the Green Bay Packers during the 1960s, when he led the team to three consecutive and five total National Football League championships in seven years. Many call him the best football coach ever.

Italian and Italian American men are usually seductively attractive and frequently charming. No wonder non-Italian women often marry them. Some of their kids become celebrities. Of course via just their fathers' surnames we don't know they're only half-Italian—which is plenty good enough!

Would you guess John Travolta is half Burke and Sylvester Stallone half Labofish? Jay Leno's mom was born a Muir (in Britain) and Robert De Niro's was an Admiral. Leonardo Di Caprio's German-born mother is an Indenbirken.

Italian speciality breads. An Italian saying says, "Buono come il pane," good as bread, and perhaps only France rivals Italy for good bread. A few examples: Tuscan and Umbrian bread has no salt but is surprisingly good just so. Moist inside, Roman bread has lots of holes and a crunchy, toasty brown crust. Rosetta is a sectioned round roll, all crust and little crumb. Scaletta are ladder-shaped, hard-wheat golden loaves from Sicily made in ovens fired with almond shells. And the pale golden bread from Altamura in Puglia is often judged Italy's finest—Romans and citizens to the north pay top prices to get hold of it.

Italian melodies are often more sweeping, sometimes even operatic, than most pop tunes. Over the decades many international pop hits have been recycled from them by changing the Italian lyrics into another language, usually without public awareness of a tune's provenance. This happens with traditional songs like "O Sole Mio" (into "It's Now or Never," most famously via Elvis Presley) and newer songs. "Grande, Grande, Grande," for instance, by Alberto Testa and Tony Renis became a #1 hit in Italy for singer Mina in 1972 but the following year was an English-language hit, if not a #1, for Shirley Bassey as "Never, Never, Never." It was also recorded by diverse singers like Julio Iglesias, Vikki Carr, Sergio Franchi, and Mireille Mathieu, and in 1997 was retitled "I Hate You Then I Love You" for Celine Dion with Luciano Pavarotti.

Italics. Reading would be duller without them. They give emphasis, without resorting to exclamation marks. Of course, some Italian Americans and even more Italians *speak* in italics. A page with too many italics can make for difficult reading; italics work best when they're the exception. They're like spices—a little goes a long way.

Jacuzzi is an internationally known name, though typically mispronounced outside Italy, where it's usually forgotten that the Italian *z* or double-*z* has a *–ts* sound as in pizza, which nobody mispronounces! Inventor Candido Jacuzzi drew inspiration "from imperial Rome, where plumbing was the most advanced and people were more cleanly (sic) than many centuries later in the Middle Ages." In 1915 in Valvasone the Jacuzzi family founded the company whose first product was a bath with massaging jets of water. Eventually the firm would employ over 4,900 people and also manufacture bathtubs, toilets, sinks, and mattresses. "Water is important," explained Candido, "but the thermal principle of heat is our big difference. The circulating hot aerated water relieves and cleanses while it soothes and stimulates—it makes people happy!"

June, July and August. Our eighth month is named after Rome's first emperor, Augustus, which means venerable or consecrated. Before that, he was just plain Octavian; his sister was Octavia, who was given in marriage to Mark

Anthony, which upset Cleopatra mightily. The eighth Roman month was October, from octo, meaning eight.

July derives from Julius Caesar, who enabled the spectacular rise of his heir Octavian.

June is from Juno, Rome's chief goddess and wife of the chief god, Jupiter—after whom the largest planet in our solar system is named. As the patroness of brides and motherhood, Juno's special month became the favorite one for weddings. The old European and Northern American tradition of bridal orange blossoms dates back to the Romans.

La Scala is the most famous opera house in the world. Ordered built by Empress Maria Theresa (the mother of Marie Antoinette), it opened in 1778, seats ca. 3,000 music lovers, and its inaugural opera was *Europe Recognized* by Antonio Salieri. La Scala's name derives from Santa Maria della Scala (St. Mary of the Staircase), a church that had occupied the same site. Virtually every great operatic composer, conductor, and singer has performed at La Scala, which was partly destroyed in World War II by bombs. Rebuilt, it opened again in 1946, less than a year after the war's end.

Lady Gaga. First the names: She was born Stefani Joanne Angelina Germanotta in New York City in 1986. A fan of Freddie Mercury and Queen, she took her performing name from the UK group's song "Radio Ga-Ga." The multiple-Grammy-winning singer-songwriter, musician, fashion provocateur, and actor who began in theatre is three-quarters Italian American, plus French Canadian. Identifying strongly with her prematurely deceased virgin aunt Joanne, Gaga believes her body houses two souls. The often androgynous chameleon also has a stage male alter ego she calls Joe Calderone.

Since her 2008 debut album *The Fame*, Gaga has been an international hit-spinner. With a vengeance. She's declared, "I've made it my goal to revolutionize pop music. The last revolution was launched by Madonna 25 years ago." The two iconoclastic Italian American divas admire each other. A generous philanthropist, Lady Gaga is also a "fierce advocate" for gay and lesbian civil rights and in 2012 founded the Born This Way Foundation to promote youth empowerment, anti-bullying, mentoring, and career development. In 2014 she collaborated with octogenarian Tony Bennett on a jazz album titled *Cheek to Cheek* which debuted at #1 on the charts.

Lake Como is hemmed in on two sides by steep green hills and lies in the shadow of the snow-covered Rhaetian Alps. It's the favorite of Italy's three stunning lakes (also Maggiore and Garda) formed at the end of the last ice age and popular with vacationers since ancient Rome. Many of its spectacular villas are home to the rich and/or famous (among them George Clooney). The lakeside villages are charming, the mountainous vistas incredible, and cafes within the remaining twelfth-century walls of the town of Como are ever chic and popular. Como is still Europe's leading producer of silk products.

Lake Lugano is shared by Switzerland and Italy, where it's sometimes called Lago Ceresio. Like the nearby, larger Lake Como, its mountain scenery is often breathtaking. Lugano is the largest city in the Italian-flavored Swiss canton of Ticino (Italian is the nation's third language, of four official ones). Lugano is Switzerland's #3 banking center after Zurich and Geneva. It's prosperous and picturesque and is the main residence of many Milanese of means.

Lamborghini was a latecomer among Italian luxury sports-car manufacturers, founded in 1963 by Ferruccio Lamborghini in Bologna to compete with Ferrari and company. His outfit earned international acclaim with its 1966 Miura sports coupe and grew quickly in its first decade, only slowing down with the 1973 oil crisis. In 1978 Lamborghini went bankrupt. Bought by Chrysler, it was later sold to a Southeast Asian group, which sold it to Volkswagen, where it remains part of VW's Audi division. Lamborghini makes both sports cars and V12 engines for offshore powerboat racing. The company symbol is a raging golden bull. Its high standards may be gauged by its 2011 workforce of 831 employees crafting only 1,711 vehicles that year. Lamborghini, which no longer produces SUVs, currently offers the V12-powered Aventador and the V10-powered Huracán.

Lancia means lance in Italian, and its original logo was a lance and shield with a flag. In 1906 racing driver Vincenzo Lancia with friend Claudio Fogolin founded Lancia and Company in Turin. It became known for innovations like being the first carmaker to produce a V4 engine, for introducing independent suspension in production cars back when live axles were standard for a car's front and rear, and for its 2013 Theta, the first production car in Europe to feature a complete electrical system as standard equipment. Many Lancia models are named with Greek-alphabet letters.

In the 1970s its Stratos, a successful rally car, boosted the firm's sporting credentials. In 2013 Antonella Bruno became CEO of Lancia, which targets women. In 2014 Lancia announced it would no longer operate outside Italy; its models are now available only within the country.

Mario Lanza has possibly been seen and heard by more people than any other operatic singer, due to the eight movies he made between 1949 and 1959, including *The Great Caruso*. He was born Alfred Arnold Cocozza (1921-1959) in South Philadelphia to immigrants from Italy's Abruzzi region. Naturally gifted, the only-child—his mother was *née* Lanza—enjoyed singing but all his life declined vocal training and discipline in general. He over-indulged in food and considered all women game. After his voice took him to Hollywood, his habits earned him a bad reputation, and by 1954's *The Student Prince* he was reduced to only singing his role while a slimmer, more responsible actor (Briton Edmund Purdom) incarnated the role. Mario's custom had been to gain lots of weight in between roles, record the soundtrack while heavy, then diet down for actual filming.

Temperamental behavior, substance abuse, and cancelled performances induced him to move to Italy in 1957, where he made his last two films and died two years later at 38.

Lasagna is one of the most beloved dishes on earth. It's also one of the oldest, and initially referred to layered casserole-type entrees that alternated pasta, sauces, and other ingredients. It may be of Greek origin. The ancient Romans had a dish named lasana or lasanum, named for the pot or container it was made in. But their lasagna differed from ours, since tomatoes come from Mexico and Europe only discovered the red fruit after Spain's conquest of Mexico in the early 1500s.

The first mention of a tomato (condemned by the Church for being "the devil's color") in a European book was in 1544 by Pietro Andrea Mattioli). The earliest English recipe to include a tomato was published in 1652.

Modern lasagna, featuring pasta, tomato sauce, meat, and cheese, apparently originated in Naples.

Latin. It's difficult to overestimate the influence of Latin on the English language. Although a Germanic language, English is far more Latinized than, say, German, Dutch, or Swedish, partly because France conquered England in 1066. As Rome's empire spread across Europe, particularly western Europe, vernacular or everyday Latin gradually evolved into French, Spanish, Portuguese, Romanian, and of course Italian. (Latin languages are sometimes referred to as Romance languages, not after romance, but Rome.)

Latin languages are spoken by a large percentage of the Western world. Latin itself lived on via the Roman Catholic Church and, for a time, in the schools. Today, Spanish is the native language of more people than any language outside Asia.

The Leaning Tower of Pisa, formerly 5.5 famous degrees askew, is the world's most famous construction mistake. The campanile is the round bell tower of Pisa's cathedral complex that includes the cathedral, baptistery, and cemetery. Construction of the tower began in 1173 but halted in 1178, at three stories. In 1278 a seventh story was achieved but work again came to a stop. In 1298 the first of several commissions was convened to investigate the tower's tilt. In 1370 it was officially completed, with a then-inclination of 1.6 degrees from vertical.

In 1934 Mussolini allowed 361 holes to be drilled into the tower's base and filled with 90 tons of cement that almost toppled the longstanding structure.

After the most recent and effective solution—a complex and costly process of soil extraction—the tower's tilt is now 3.99 degrees and it's set for a few more centuries.

"If you want a photograph that will impress everybody who sees it," offers two-time Oscar-winner Roberto Benigni, "when you are in Pisa with the Leaning Tower in the far background, stand sideways and lean forward a little, bend one knee, and raise your arms high with the palms outward…ask your photographer to stand at the correct angle to you and the building so it looks like you are holding up the Leaning Tower of Pisa. This makes the most wonderful picture you will ever take in all your travels."

> Most every schoolchild has heard of the experiment Galileo Galilei conducted from the bell tower by simultaneously dropping two objects of unequal weight to see if the heavier one would land first. Galileo did lecture as a young mathematics professor at the University of Pisa (which opened in 1343), but the experiment story is apocryphal.

Christopher Lee's full name is Christopher Frank Carandini Lee, born in 1922 and Sir Christopher since 2009. His maternal great-grandmother was opera singer Marie Carandini, whose husband was an Italian political refugee. The 6'5" actor became a star portraying Dracula and other horror figures for Britain's Hammer Films. A rare non-Hammer starring role was the title role in the James Bond opus *The Man With the Golden Gun* as assassin Francisco Scaramanga. Lee also appeared in the *Star Wars*, *Lord of the Rings*, and *Hobbit* franchises.

"I've always enjoyed singing, which is part of my heritage," noted Lee. From 1986 to 1998 he recorded several operatic and other musical pieces—including symphonic metal!—and in 2010, having collaborated with assorted metal bands since 2005, he received the Spirit of Metal award at the Metal Hammer Golden God awards ceremony.

Leghorn chickens originated in Tuscany and were first exported to the U.S. in 1828 from the Tuscan port of Livorno, which in the sixteenth and seventeenth centuries was called Legorno, thus it's Leghorn in English. In demand for the white eggs they laid so prolifically—an average of 280 eggs a year—the chickens were originally called "Italians" but by 1865 were renamed after their port of embarkation. In 1870 they were introduced to Britain via the United States, and today most people don't know this popular poultry breed came from Italy.

One of the more indelible Warner Bros. animated characters during the golden age of cartoons was Foghorn Leghorn, a large, aggressive but lovable white Southern rooster. Go figure.

Lemon houses. Lemons are believed to have been imported from the port of Genoa to Gargnano on Lake Garda's shore during the thirteenth century. Lemons were usually grown farther south, but the lake's climate was temperate, and by the eighteenth century hundreds of thousands of lemons were being exported to Germany and Russia. They were tended in hundreds of limonaie—lemon houses comprising tall, slender stone pillars upholding wooden latticework over which glass sheets kept the frosts off the citrus.

The lemon business began dying out in the late 1800s on account of disease and artificial citric acid. Restored lemon houses are now open to visitors.

A few miles from Gargnano, also on Lake Garda, is Salo, named in 1943 the capital of the Social Republic of Italy—also known as the Republic of Salo—in an attempt by Mussolini and Hitler to reorganize Fascism under the threat of American forces advancing from the south.

Lentils in Italy were considered only poor people's food until World War II and its shortages. Thereafter they were more highly regarded and willingly consumed—traditionally, on New Year's Day for good luck. They may be eaten hot or cold, in soups or salads, as an accompaniment to sausage, or in Pasta e Lenticchie, a mixture of ditalini (a short, tubular pasta that means "little toes," often used in soup) and lentils.

Leonardo is widely held to be history's greatest genius. Da Vinci's (1452-1519) interests and talents seemed to cover every field of endeavor, and his ideas and insights prefigured more modern discoveries and inventions than anyone else's. Though he considered himself chiefly a painter, Leonardo spent surprisingly little time painting—yet one of only three portraits he did became the most famous painting ever—for he pursued so many interests and projects.

The appearance of things and how they worked consumed much of the polymath's time and interest. A superb draftsman, he was able to illustrate his discoveries as nobody had previously done, in his now-revered notebooks with the backwards "mirror handwriting" (Microsoft's Bill Gates paid $40 million for a portion of the notebooks). Leonardo believed his acquired knowledge would make him a better painter, whether it involved studying the movement of water, the flight of birds, the growth of plants, human anatomy, gears and gear trains, pumps, weapons, or a myriad of other phenomena.

Famed as the birthplace of Leonardo, the hilltop town of Vinci's thirteenth-century castle houses the Museo Leonardiano (ca. 28 miles/42 km. from Florence). It features wooden models of Leonardo's machines and inventions, most based on drawings from his notebooks, copies of which accompany the models. The term "Renaissance man" was coined to describe da Vinci and his multifaceted genius. Besides painting, sculpture, and architecture, Leonardo was a man of science who vigorously studied the natural and physical sciences, mechanics, engineering, mathematics, and more.

The museum's da Vincian models include a bicycle, his conception of an automobile, of a helicopter, an armored tank, and a machine gun, centuries before the unfortunate fact.

> Da Vinci's half-brother Bartolomeo (Leonardo reportedly had 17 half-siblings), wishing to replicate a genius, married a peasant from the village of Leonardo's mother (Leonardo was "illegitimate"). The resultant

> son, Pierino da Vinci, born in 1529 or 1530, became a painter and sculptor, as intended. He was good enough that some of his work was temporarily misattributed to Leonardo's arch-rival Michelangelo. Because Pierino died of malarial fever at age 23, the ultimate extent of his artistic talent would never be known.

Ruggero Leoncavallo, whose surname means lion-horse, wrote his first opera at age 18 but is best known for the 1892 one-act opera *I Pagliacci* (The Clowns), a tale of love, jealousy, and murder performed more naturalistically than was usual. Its high point is the celebrated aria "Vesti la Giubba" (Put On the Costume), in which the bitter, cuckolded clown laughs through his tears. Enrico Caruso's 1902 recording of the song was the first million-selling record in history.

Alas, success seldom visited the Neapolitan Leoncavallo (1858-1919), who'd planned to finance his first opera with his own savings, except that his producer fled with the funds, reducing the youth to earning his bread performing music in coffeehouses.

Later, his friend Giacomo Puccini stole Ruggero's idea for another opera, which became the hit *La Boheme*. Leoncavallo's opera of the same name opened after Puccini's, and wilted in its shadow. With producers and friends like those….

Sergio Leone was a frankly commercial director, producer and screenwriter. Most closely associated with spaghetti westerns and gangster films, the Roman (1929-1989) declined to direct *The Godfather* in favor of his own gangster epic, *Once Upon a Time in America* (1984). Starring Robert De Niro, it consumed years of Leone's time; Warner Bros. trimmed his four-hour version to two hours, but it flopped anyway.

In the 1950s, Sergio, who'd been an assistant to Vittorio de Sica, penned sword-and-sandal screenplays. His directorial bow had him replacing Mario Bonnard, who was too ill to helm *The Last Days of Pompeii* (1959), starring Steve "Hercules" Reeves, an American made a star in Italy.

Leone's signature style often alternated extreme close-ups with lengthy long shots. "Subtlety," he declared. "I can't even pronounce it."

The Leopard (Il Gattopardo) is known to most non-Italians only via the lavish 1963 Luchino Visconti film starring Burt Lancaster, Claudia Cardinale, and Alain Delon. However, in Italy the novel by Giuseppe Tomasi, Duke of Palma and Prince of Lampedusa (1896-1957), is a national epic on a par with *Gone with the Wind* in the United States. Tomasi was part of the fading Sicilian aristocracy that heralded back to the Norman eleventh century and ended in 1860 when Garibaldi ejected the Bourbons from Italy. It was about this transition and these once-privileged characters trying to fit into the new order that Tomasi wrote.

As Tomasi lay on his deathbed, his manuscript was sent anonymously to a female writer-editor in Rome who didn't read it. It then reached a Milanese publisher who passed it to a Sicilian novelist who read it, deemed it too "essayish," and wrote to the failing Tomasi to tell him so. Tomasi died, but then a novelist-editor to whom the female writer had sent the manuscript traveled to Palermo and at the late prince's home found another manuscript in the author's handwriting that included important additions to the novel—and that was the version brought to light by the Feltrinelli publishing house of Milan in 1958. It became the top-selling novel in Italian history.

The English title is a misnomer. Leopard in Italian is leopardo. Gattopardo means serval, a wild cat that appears on the Tomasi family's coat of arms.

Primo Levi wrote what the Royal Institution of Great Britain termed "the best science book ever written," *The Periodic Table* (1975), about the qualities of chemical elements but also much more. Although the Mussolini regime in 1938 banned Jews from attending institutions of higher learning, Levi (1919-1987) was able to obtain a degree in chemistry in 1941. Then in 1944 he was arrested as a member of the anti-Fascist resistance and deported to Auschwitz.

The Turin-born Holocaust survivor is best known for his non-technical books, novels, short stories, and essays. His most famous work, *If This Is a Man* (English title *Survival in Auschwitz*), was the first part of an autobiographical trilogy.

Levi declared, "After Auschwitz, I had an absolute need to write. Not only as a moral duty, but as a psychological need." Levi, who wrote poetry for the Turin newspaper *La Stampa*, continued his career as a chemist, working almost three decades at a Turin paint company.

Rita Levi-Montalcini was the oldest then-living Nobel Prize winner in 2012 when she died at 103. Born in Turin in 1909, she became a doctor. Her husband, a professor, was also Jewish, and in Mussolini's Fascist Italy of 1938 both were fired from their jobs. They continued their experiments in embryology in a lab in their bedroom, studying the interiors of eggs in the a.m. and consuming them in the p.m. In 1947 Levi-Montalcini emigrated to the U.S., where she did research at Washington University in St. Louis.

In 1949 she discovered that embryos create more nerve cells than required by growing tissues, leading to her discovery of factors which control nerve and skin growth. Upon her return to Italy, she became director of the cell-biology laboratory at the University of Rome, where her pioneering research in the neurophysiology of senile dementia resulted in a Nobel Prize in 1986.

Life Is Beautiful (1997) starred and was written, directed, and produced by irrepressible comic Roberto Benigni. Lauded, lambasted, and successful—the movie won Academy Awards for Best Foreign Language Film and

Best Actor—*La Vita è Bella* depicts life for one Italian family (a Jewish father, Christian mother, and their small son) under Mussolini and his ally Hitler. The movie's second half presents father and son surviving in a concentration camp. Comedy is employed to confront reality, and though this view of the Holocaust seems to focus on survivors, at film's end it is revealed that Guido (Benigni) has died.

Life With Luigi is a little- but fondly-remembered CBS-radio sitcom which aired from 1948 to 1953 and centered on Luigi Basco, a newly naturalized immigrant adjusting to life in Chicago, living in a rooming house and taking English classes. The show's framing device was the weekly letter he composed to "Dear Mamma Mia" back home in Italy. Luigi was voiced by "the man of a thousand accents," J. Carrol Naish, who portrayed him on the TV version that was soon retitled *The Little Immigrant* and recast with the more petite Vito Scotti but which still failed (television's sitcom characters were moving out to the suburbs, and ethnic was no longer "in").

Virna Lisi created a lasting impression when, Venus-like, she popped out of a cake and married Jack Lemmon in *How to Murder Your Wife* (1964). Born Virna Lisa Pieralisi in 1936 in Ancona, she bowed in Italian films in 1953 and went international with the wide distribution of *Romulus* *and Remus* (1961). Despite her ravishing blonde beauty and a lengthy filmography including numerous foreign films, Lisi didn't achieve the top rank of stardom but did mature into a talented actress, playing the diabolic (and brunette) Catherine de Medici in the French epic *Queen Margot* in 1994. She has won at the Cannes Film Festival and at France's Cesar and Italy's David di Donatello Awards.

Gina Lollobrigida (first name: Luigina, female for Luigi) was born in 1927 in Subiaco, not far from Rome. She debuted onscreen in 1946 and by 1955 was starring in *La Donna Piu Bella del Mondo* (*The Most Beautiful Woman in the World*). The next year "La Lollo" went Hollywood with *Trapeze*, as she who comes between best buddies Burt Lancaster and Tony Curtis. In the 1960s she was as high-profile as Sophia Loren. An intergalactic-beauty-contest episode of TV's animated *The Jetsons* featured Gina Lollo-Jupiter and a curly Italian lettuce was named Lollo after her.

From the mid '70s Gina wound down her acting career and turned to photography and sculpting. She kept her looks well into her eighties and in 2013 sold her jewelry collection, donating the almost $5 million raised to stem-cell therapy research.

Lollobrigida's 1968 vehicle *Buona Sera, Mrs. Campbell* provided the unofficial storyline for the ABBA musical *Mamma Mia!*

> Movies can be instructive. This writer's mother took my sister and I to a re-release of *Where the Hot Wind Blows* (1958), starring Lollobrigida, Mastroianni, Yves Montand, and Melina Mercouri. Months later, after we three got out of the car my mother found she'd left her car keys inside the locked car—and didn't want our father to know, when he came home. Fortunately she'd left the driver's window open an inch or so and I remembered what Gina had done in that movie. I got a coat hanger, worked it down into the car and wriggled it until it caught the door handle…ecco! We opened the car door and retrieved Mama's keys.

Guy Lombardo (1902-1977) was known as Mr. New Year's Eve. For nearly half a century the band leader and his Royal Canadians rang in the New Year via big-band remotes on radio (starting in 1928) and then television, including a live segment from New York's Times Square. He was born Gaetano Alberto Lombardo in London, Ontario, the son of immigrants. His tailor father, an amateur singer, had four of his five sons learn a musical instrument—"Guy" played the violin.

The Royal Canadians, who included brothers Carmen, Lebert, Victor, and other musicians, played what they called

"The Sweetest Music This Side of Heaven" and sold 100 to 300 million records. It was Guy Lombardo who made a New Year's Eve media tradition of playing the Scottish "Auld Lang Syne." But by the mid 1970s he and his band were facing increased and younger competition, specifically Dick Clark. However, CBS still aired the Royal Canadians for two years after Lombardo's death.

Lombardy poplar (*Populus nigra italica*) is an elegant black Italian poplar with a unique tall, column-like silhouette. Andy Warhol entertained the notion of doing a series of paintings of this tree. Its buds were long used for treating colds, sinusitis, arthritis, rheumatism, muscular pain, and dry skin. They can also be placed in hot water for use as an inhalant to relieve congested nasal passages.

Sophia. Once, her first name was enough. Everyone knew Italy's biggest movie star. Few performers have ever shone as brilliantly and fetchingly as la Loren. Besides that face, that figure, that voice, and that laugh, the former Sofia Scicolone of Pozzuoli, near Naples, had talent, winning the Academy Award for *Two Women* (1960) and decades later an honorary Oscar.

The actress's last name was changed for international audiences, after that of Norwegian star Marta Toren, who later died in her early thirties. However, the women's surnames stressed different syllables.

> Sophia Loren recalled, "My mother was beautiful—an Italian Garbo. Romilda wanted so much to be an actress. She let her parents prevent her....Without my mother, I would not have become a star. Her dream was mine. So I feel like three people: Sofia the grown-up girl, Sophia the movie star, and Romilda the movie star."
>
> Loren starred in the 2010 TV mini-series *My House Is Full of Mirrors* in the role of her mother, who'd won a Garbo-look-alike contest. A younger actress played Sofia/Sophia.

Lorenzo the Magnificent (1448-1492). There was virtually no democracy in those days, so how admired could any leader really be? However, apart from being a skillful diplomat, a would-be peacemaker, a magnate, and a generous patron of the arts who sponsored Michelangelo and Botticelli, among others, the Florentine leader was a poet whose lovelorn verse remains popular. Example: "Thus did a lady take my heart; nor she wants nor gives it back; a noose around it has she cast; sets me on fire, she burns me black!"

And: "O give me peace at last, passionate sighs, ye thoughts upon that beauteous face transfixed, that tranquil sleep might somehow be welcomed to these my sorrowful, watery eyes."

Macaroni is from maccheroni, which in the eighteenth century mostly supplanted vermicelli (literally, little worms), the centuries-old name for non-stuffed pasta. Macaroni-and-cheese recipes date back to the late thirteenth century. Macaroni referred to both straight and curved pasta, but in the U.S. the word (which is plural) eventually specified hollow elbow-shaped pasta. In colonial New England the dish was sometimes called macaroni pudding and used Parmesan, later switching to Cheddar cheese. Some U.S. sources credit Thomas Jefferson's daughter Mary Randolph with "inventing" modern mac 'n cheese via a "pasta machine" that her father—whose official hostess she became after his wife died—brought back from a visit to Italy. Randolph's 1824 cookbook *The Virginia Housewife* includes her macaroni recipe with Parmesan cheese.

In 1937, before the Great Depression had ended, Kraft put macaroni and cheese into a box. It yielded a cheap, easy, and tasty meal and was an instant success. Mac 'n cheese—warm, gooey, aromatic, and delicious—was and is a classic comfort food.

Madonna. This euphonious and elegant word means my lady. It often comes off classier than its French counterpart, madame, which sometimes sounds ageist or (in most places outside Nevada) illegal.

Prima donna means first lady, an opera company's female lead—now additionally a temperamental female opera star, also known as a diva. Although the terms have migrated into English, their male equivalents, primo uomo and divo, have not.

Donna is simply a classic though currently out-of-fashion name for a girl, woman, or lady.

The Madonna Inn is one of the most unique hostelries anywhere. It graces—some say gaudily—the outskirts of San Luis Obispo in central California, and was founded in 1958 by construction millionaire Alex Madonna, who disliked boxy motels and cloned rooms. "Anyone can build one room and 1,000 like it," he said. "I want people to come in with a smile and leave with a smile. It's fun."

Each of the original 12 rooms was very individually designed. Within a year Madonna had 40 rooms. Word of mouth was his best advertising. Today there are 110 pricey and unforgettably decorated rooms with themes like Daisy Mae, Elegance, Safari Room, Irish Hills, Kona Rock, Austrian Suite, Caveman Room, and Hearts and Flowers. The motel includes a restaurant and bakery, its common rooms feature bountiful pink roses, western murals, and hammered copper, and the men's room boasts a rock waterfall urinal. The Madonna Inn's exterior is faux Swiss Alps, and it has appeared in various TV programs and films, including the *Rigoletto* segment of the opera-themed movie *Aria* (1987).

Anna Magnani (1908-1973), Italy's top star following World War II, won international acclaim in Rossellini's *Rome:*

Open City (1945), the neorealist film that drew Ingrid Bergman to Italy, away from artificial and often irrelevant Hollywood moviemaking. An accomplished stage actress, Magnani befriended playwright Tennessee Williams and starred in the 1955 movie of his *The Rose Tattoo*. It earned her a surprise Academy Award, for she was neither young nor a beauty and was foreign. Actor Ward Bond, John Wayne's drinking buddy and fellow McCarthy-era communist witchhunter, grumbled that they were called "the Oscars, not the raviolis."

Hollywood called twice more—another Williams adaptation and *Wild Is the Wind*, which brought another Oscar nomination. Anna then returned to Italy and worked less often on screen. Her final appearance was a cameo in *Fellini Roma* (1972). Born into poverty and raised in dire circumstances, the passionate star's death occasioned a degree of national mourning usually reserved for a pope.

Henry Mancini (1924-1994) was born Enrico Nicola Mancini in Cleveland, the son of immigrants—his steelworker father played the flute. Henry, whose last name would be permanently mispronounced, helped personalize movie scores in the 1960s, eschewing the often symphonic sound of prior Hollywood films. He won four Academy Awards and 29 Grammys and sold some 30 million records. Among his songs and scores: "Moon River," "Days of Wine and Roses," "Dear Heart," "Whistling Away the Dark," "Baby Elephant

Walk," "The Pink Panther," "Two for the Road," "Sunflower," "Charade," and "Victor/Victoria."

Silvana Mangano (1930-1989), a half-English beauty born in Rome, wasn't as ambitious as Loren or Lollobrigida, and her husband, producer Dino De Laurentiis, tended to give her films short shrift in comparison to his own, unlike Loren's producer husband Carlo Ponti. *Bitter Rice* (1949) made Mangano a star. In movies from 1945 to 1987, Silvana shone in both stellar and smaller roles, including *Gold of Naples*, *Ulysses*, *Teorema*, *Dark Eyes*, *Death in Venice*, and *Dune*.

Mangano and De Laurentiis eventually divorced, but had four children during the course of their marriage, including movie producer Raffaella. Granddaughter Giada De Laurentiis became a host on cable-TV's Food Network. Silvana Mangano died of cancer at 59. De Laurentiis remarried and had more children.

Mangia! So eat already, caro. Befitting a country with possibly the best cuisine in the world, eating is an Italian national pastime and also something of an obsession. It's said if you're not hungry, an Italian may tell you to eat something to make you hungry. Mamma's food is often considered more healing than a doctor's medicine.

Cooking, eating, and drinking coffee and wine might be said to be Italy's *raison d'être*. Growing at least a portion of one's own fresh vegetables and fruits is considered far more than a hobby, and little girls—increasingly, also little boys—are taught early to replicate their mothers' culinary specialties.

Manicotti isn't that common but is that delicious. It's made with tubular pasta or maccheroni four to five inches long filled with ricotta cheese and ham and served with tomato sauce, sometimes baked. The name comes from *manica*, Latin for sleeve.

A variation of manicotti uses white besciamella sauce, usually with Romano or Parmesan cheese, or a red sauce. The filling, besides ricotta, may or may not include ground meat but features spinach, and may be called cannelloni, which means large tubes, from cannello, tube.

Andrea Mantegna (1431-1506) was a great artist but went from being a poor woodworker's son to the first Renaissance court painter due to his political skills. From 1460 until his death he was employed by the Gonzagas of Mantua, who wished to be regarded as glorious rulers and munificent patrons of the arts. So he painted them as heroes, descendants of ancient and mythical beings, whether human, superhuman, or divine. Leonardo, Michelangelo, Raphael, and Bramante all succeeded Mantegna as court painters for powerful patrons.

Alessandro Manzoni (1785-1873) was born into an affluent family and had the leisure to become possibly the greatest nineteenth-century Italian novelist. His *magnum opus* was titled *The Betrothed*. Set during fictional plague times, it bravely dealt with Italian nationalism during a period when the country was largely under foreign control. Manzoni's lifelong dream was a united Italy, which he lived to see, and his hope was one language that would unite the nation—to which end he eschewed his Milanese dialect in favor of a standard national language based primarily on Tuscan.

Maraschino. The neon-red cherry that decorates ice cream sundaes, milkshakes, cocktails, etc., is named for the marasca cherry from Croatia's Dalmatian coast. However there's also Maraschino, the clear, slightly bitter liqueur first produced by Venetian entrepreneur Francesco Drioli in 1759, when Dalmatia was a possession of the Venetian republic. Sold in squarish green bottles made in Murano glass factories, it became popular throughout Europe by the late eighteenth century. In the twentieth century an investment group from Milan bought the business and after World War II discontinued the historic liqueur.

Congressman Vito Marcantonio explained, "Most Americans of Italian heritage are Democrats because our families have experienced minor or major discrimination for our background, our religion, or even our ancestral language." Disheartened by the tight WASP control of both political parties, Marcantonio (1902-1954) joined the more liberal American Labor Party, founded in 1936 and for a decade quite successful, repeatedly electing Representative Marcantonio and delivering, via New York's open-primary system, hundreds of thousands of votes for President Franklin Delano Roosevelt, Mayor Fiorello LaGuardia, and Rep. Adam Clayton Powell.

In 1944 a more conservative faction split off from the ALP, which lost steam after Marcantonio's premature death and suffered the rise of McCarthyism's political witch-hunts and smear campaigns. The ALP officially dissolved in 1956.

Guglielmo Marconi (1874-1937) was, alas, a devout Fascist. But at age 20 the Bologna-born Irish Italian (his mother was *née* Jameson, his father was an aristocrat) created a device to transmit sound without using wires. The next year, he extended his invention's range to one mile, eventually patenting the "wireless" and establishing the Marconi Company in England. In 1901 a wireless message was transmitted across the Atlantic between Britain and Canada, and in 1909 won Marconi a Nobel Prize for Physics.

Marconi's claim of inventing radio, which took off in the 1920s the way television did in the 1950s, began unraveling after his death. In 1943 the U.S. Supreme Court finally recognized Serbian American inventor Nikola Tesla as the first to actually conceive and patent the principles of radio, and struck down Marconi's fundamental patent. Tesla's first patent was in 1897; Marconi's first patent attempt was turned down in 1900.

Jerry Maren (*né* Gerard Marenghi in 1920) is a 4'3" midget actor and the only surviving cast member of *The Wizard of Oz* (1939). He was the center Munchkin of the three-man Lollipop Guild who hands Dorothy (Judy Garland) a welcoming lollipop. Jerry was one of 12 children, the others all average-sized. Better known for his commercial characters than movies, Jerry incarnated Buster Brown (selling shoes) on radio and TV, was Little Oscar for the Oscar Mayer Co., and played Mayor McCheese in McDonald's ads. In 2008 he published his memoirs, *Short and Sweet* (this writer had the pleasure of interviewing him), and in 2013 pressed his hand- and footprints into the forecourt of Grauman's Chinese Theatre in Hollywood.

Another Italian midget, Olga Nardone, was the center Munchkin of the Lullabye League, female counterpart to the Lollipop Guild.

Marietto, the child actor born Carlo Angeletti in 1947, would merit inclusion here even if he'd only appeared in one delightful film, *It Started in Naples* (1960), as Sophia Loren's nephew Nando. Clark Gable, as the boy's uncle, wants to take Nando to America (from Capri) until Gable falls in love with Sophia and Italy. Between 1958 and 1964 Marietto did 11 Italian, Hollywood, German, and French movies. His last was *Behold a Pale Horse*, director Fred Zinnemann's unsuccessful Spanish Civil War story starring Gregory Peck. In his 1992 memoirs Zinnemann said Angeletti had become a medical doctor.

Marsala wine. Italy's most famous fortified wine is named after the Sicilian port that in the late 1700s shipped it to England, where it became widely popular. Alcohol was added to guarantee its lasting the long sea voyage. Marsala has remained fortified—with brandy or neutral grape spirit—because foreign markets prefer it so, though Sicilians often drink "vintage." Aged in wooden caskets, the dark, sweet dessert wine comes in three shades—gold, amber, ruby—and uses, among others, Grillo, Inzolia, and Catarratto white grapes.

Marsala was originally an aperitif (via Latin *aperire*, to open… the appetite) served between first and second courses. Now chilled Marsala is often served with cheeses, fruits, or pastries.

> Culinarily, it's especially popular in U.S. restaurants, where a rich, caramelized sauce is achieved by reducing the wine nearly to syrup, then adding onions, mushrooms, and herbs. Chicken Marsala, a classic, comprises flour-coated chicken cutlets braised in a combination of Marsala, butter, olive oil, mushrooms, and spices—sometimes served with red potatoes and red and green bell peppers.
>
> Marsala is also used in some risotto dishes and in rich Italian desserts like tiramisu, zabaglione, and shortcake.

The Marshalls' paternal surname was Masciarelli until Garry and Penny's father changed it before they were born (his family was from San Martino sulla Marrucina in Abruzzo). Both siblings acted but wound up very successful movie directors—Penny, born in 1943 in New York City, was the first female to helm a film that grossed $100 million (twice): *Big* and *A League of Their Own*.

Garry, born in 1934, early on moved into writing for television, then produced TV series like *The Odd Couple* and *Happy Days*. Penny got her acting break on the former sitcom before costarring in the top-rated *Laverne and Shirley*, a *Happy Days* spin-off. Prior to her brother's connections, her most widely seen effort was a commercial for beautiful hair; Penny played the girl with ugly hair. The other girl was Farrah Fawcett.

Garry had major movie hits with *Pretty Woman*, *Beaches*, *Runaway Bride*, *The Princess Diaries,* and its sequel.

Martello towers were small round forts numerously erected along England's coastline for defense during the Napoleonic wars when Napoleon sought to add Britain to his empire. Ironically, they were named after one such tower at Cape Mortella (sic) in Corsica that the British captured with difficulty in 1794.

Dean Martin, born Dino Crocetti, reportedly had a reductive nose job (financed by mentor Lou Costello of Abbott and Costello) that allowed him to become a matinee idol. Dean once quipped, "You want big noses, go to Italy and turn south, way south." Originally teamed with comic Jerry Lewis, Martin (1917-1995) was a bigger success on his own, starring in movies and for a long time selling more records than fellow Rat Packer Frank Sinatra. He also owned Dino's on the Sunset Strip in Los Angeles and segued into a long-running TV variety series. Though his image was tinged with alcohol, Martin was an undemanding professional, and it was said the martini glasses he often held in public were usually filled with Evian water.

Dino recorded several Italian-flavored songs, most famously "That's Amore," which comic actor Vito Scotti called "the unofficial Italian American anthem."

Martini is both a branded Italian vermouth and a cocktail employing gin and dry vermouth and garnished with an olive or twist of lemon. In 1929 Martini and Rossi registered their famous red-ball-and-bar logo. The company, which branched out into sparkling wine (e.g., Asti), began in the nineteenth century in Pessione as a vermouth bottling plant. The martini was the leading cocktail of mid-twentieth century America. Thereafter it was viewed as old-fashioned until it was redefined as a classic. Shaken or stirred.

Chico Marx (1887-1961) was Leonard Marx, oldest of the Marx Brothers. Pre-Hollywood, the siblings were vaudeville stars. A working-class medium, vaudeville relished ethnic humor and stereotypes partly because much of the audience was foreign-born. Chico—pronounced Chicko—always played Italian and used an accent. His persona was a friendly con man, usually in cahoots with silent brother Harpo. Chico once declared, "I've been Italian so long, I almost believe it myself now, even if all my brothers are Jewish too."

Mascarpone is a soft, fresh cow's milk cheese near to butter's consistency but with less butterfat. It's a dessert cheese, enjoyed on crackers, bread, sometimes cake, or of course in desserts like tiramisu. The best mascarpone reputedly comes from Lombardy and Emilia-Romagna. It's mentioned as far back as 1168, and the name may derive from mascherare, meaning to dress up, though mascarpa is a dialect word for ricotta, which resembles mascarpone.

Maserati brothers Alfieri, Bindo, Carlo, Ettore, and Ernesto had a passion for fast cars and eventually built and sold race cars. In 1914 Alfieri founded the Maserati car company in Bologna. Its logo, a trident, was based by artist brother Mario on that of Neptune in a famous local fountain. The company's tagline is "Luxury, sports and style cast in exclusive cars"—with bespoke interiors, yet. In 1940 corporate headquarters moved to and remain in Modena. For years, Maserati's arch rival was Ferrari, which bought Maserati in 1997—both are now owned by FIAT. The Maserati division is selling more cars than ever but keeps a cap on quantity and maintains high quality. It recently offered two four-door sedans in its lineup at once for the first time, and in 2015 introduced the Maserati Levante, its first SUV.

Marcello Mastroianni (1924-1996) was easily the most famous male Italian movie star. Captured by the Germans and sent to a concentration camp, he escaped and hid in Venice until World War II was over. In 1947 he began his movie career (brother Ruggero became a film editor), eventually working for directors Visconti, Fellini, Antonioni, and De Sica. Fellini made him an international star with *La Dolce Vita* (1960) and *8½* (1962, the basis of the stage musical and movie *Nine*). Son of a carpenter and nephew of a sculptor, Marcello carved out a gallery of characters from union organizer, glutton, and several hedonists to a murder-minded husband in *Divorce, Italian Style*, a priest who wishes to marry in *The Priest's Wife* (with Sophia Loren), and a gay man persecuted by Mussolini's Fascists in *A Special Day*, which yielded an Oscar nomination.

The May King. Italy's "May King" Umberto II (1904-1983) ruled from May 9 to June 2, 1946. The May King was Italy's last king. He went into exile when Italy, via referendum, chose to become a republic. The House of Savoy was the longest ruling dynasty in Europe, starting with the first count of Savoy (980-ca. 1048) Umberto I Biancamano (White Hand). In the 1800s the dynasty united Italy's city states into a parliamentary monarchy, completing the process by World War I.

Despite marriage and four children—the only son was often said to have been fathered by Air Force Minister Italo Balbo—Umberto II was persistently rumored to be gay. The facts came out after his death. His lovers had included director Luchino Visconti, actor Jean Marais, and boxer Primo Carnera. When Umberto left Italy for exile in Portugal his wife—it had been an arranged marriage—moved to France and Switzerland; she died in the latter country in 2001.

Filippo Mazzei, with his neighbor Thomas Jefferson, planted the first vineyard in the United States. Born in 1730 near

Florence, Mazzei was a doctor who'd moved to London, where he met Benjamin Franklin and agreed to move to the British colonies in 1773. With George Washington's encouragement, he returned to Italy in 1779 to secretly purchase and transport arms to the new nation's military. After revisiting the U.S. in 1785, Mazzei wrote a history of the American Revolution published in Paris in 1788, and then participated in the French Revolution, which began in 1789, finally dying in Pisa in 1816.

Giuseppe Mazzini. Of the triumvirate behind the unification of Italy, the visionary and organizer was the slim, charismatic, Genoa-born Mazzini (1805-1872), who believed Italians "ought to struggle for liberty of country." He habitually wore black in mourning for the disunity of his country. Progressive in outlook, Mazzini envisioned a democratic republic, though it turned out to be a monarchy, for which he declined to take an oath of allegiance. In 1848-1849 when the pope's rule in Rome was temporarily ended, Mazzini became the equivalent of president of the Roman Republic. In the 1860s, after Italy was one nation, he was elected to Parliament but the right-center government refused to seat him. Mazzini grew disillusioned with politics when he saw that even under a single government, the majority of Italians were still poorly served by their leaders.

> By financing some of Mazzini's pro-unification activities, Princess Cristina Trivulzio Barbiano del Belgioioso (1808-1871) was forced to flee to France where she underwrote and edited Italian nationalist publications. Once returned to Milan, she headed an 1848 plot to end Austrian rule in northern Italy before traveling to Rome to help Mazzini and Garibaldi, who'd expelled the pope and declared a (short-lived) republic that ended in 1849. This time Princess Cristina fled to Turkey where she bought a farm, returning to Milan in 1859 after the Austrians were gone. Reluctantly she supported the Savoy monarchy as Italy's best hope for unification.

Melanzane, eggplants or aubergines, are more versatile than generally thought and well appreciated in Italy. They were cultivated in India, from whence they reached the Middle East and were introduced to Europe—through Spain and Sicily—by Arab invaders. As food historian Gillian Riley put it, melanzane are "transmogrified into gleaming oily morsels, sprinkled with flashes of green herbs, tides of red tomato, and pale molten cheese." Melanzane alla Parmigiana is a national favorite. The vegetable may be grilled, floured and fried, stuffed and roasted, or cubed and cooked al funghetto, meaning sliced as one does with mushrooms.

Improved breeds have deleted eggplants' mild bitterness and have skins ranging from deep purple to streaked violet and white and shapes including oval, long, or round.

Giancarlo Menotti (1911-2007) was born in Milan but arrived in the U.S. at 16 and became the most successful American opera composer (which some cynics said isn't saying that much). He's perhaps best known for launching an opera festival in Spoleto, Italy, in 1958 that in the 1980s expanded to performances in Charleston, South Carolina—also known as the Festival of the Two Worlds.

Antonio Meucci. Did he, rather than Alexander Graham Bell, invent the telephone? The Florence-born Meucci (1808-1889) sued Bell in 1886, and the U.S. attorney eventually charged Bell with patent fraud. The criminal case finally ended with the death of Meucci, now virtually forgotten. An emigrant to Cuba and then the U.S., Meucci was employed behind the scenes in the theatre but worked consistently on his pet experiment, the "telephone."

He'd found a way to improve the galvanization of metals, devised a crude form of electroshock therapy, and accidentally created a primitive telephone. By 1855 he had a working model of his invention, demonstrating it publicly in 1860. But while sick in the hospital, Meucci's wife sold all his papers and models for $6, to raise money to pay his bills.

So he had to begin again from scratch. He was ready by 1870 but couldn't raise the exorbitant $250 patent fee that worked against most immigrants and others with minimal resources. He sought the help of the Western Union Telegraph Company, but his papers and documents got "lost"—reportedly the same papers filed by Bell in 1876 to patent the telephone as his own invention.

"Mezzogiorno," or mid-day, is the name frequently applied to Italy's South. It entered currency in the 1700s and may derive from the Latin *meridies*, used to mean south because of the sun's position at mid-day (in the Northern Hemisphere). Garibaldi popularized "Mezzogiorno," and after Italy's unification it became quasi-official.

Michelangelo (1475-1564) is usually known minus his surname of Buonarroti. Everyone knows he was an artistic genius—in sculpture (*David*, the *Pietá*, *Moses*), painting (the Sistine Chapel), and architecture (much of St. Peter's Cathedral). He was also a gifted poet who composed enduring sonnets and madrigals. As a personality, he was impatient, often tactless, proud, and jealous, especially of Leonardo da Vinci, 23 years his senior, with whom he competed in Florence. Historian Barbara Tuchman noted, "As a genius, Michelangelo knew his worth and believed he should stand alone. He bitterly resented that his light should be dimmed by a yet greater and more varied genius."

> Buonarroti dedicated some 30 love sonnets to Tommaso dei Cavalieri, a handsome young nobleman who was the object of his greatest affection. Platonic or otherwise, their relationship endured; Tommaso was present at Michelangelo's death 32 years after they met. Some of the poems were published in 1623—with the pronouns changed. The misrepresentation was corrected by Englishman John Addington Symonds, who translated the original poems and in 1893 published a two-volume biography of the artist.
>
> Michelangelo's sonnets were the first surviving major group of poems since the classical era to be written by one man to another—over 50 years before Shakespeare's *Fair Youth* sequence, including "Sonnet 18" that begins, "Shall I compare thee to a summer's day?"

Milan has a work-obsessed reputation in the rest of the country. But there's more to the northern metropolis than Italy's stock exchange, its fashion headquarters, one of

Europe's largest trade-fair complexes, skyscrapers (including the Pirelli building, an early classic), and Expo 2015, which turned the world's spotlight on Italy's industrial powerhouse. There is also the Duomo, Milan's spectacular Gothic cathedral; opera at La Scala, priceless art, Lombard cuisine, love of calcio (soccer), rollicking nightlife, elegant shopping and arcades, and a love of—besides money—beauty and history.

Milanese and milanesa. Milanese is the adjective for Milano, also a native of Milan or in the style of Milan, and specifically and gastronomically a food item coated with flour or bread crumbs and browned in butter or hot oil. Regarding pasta, Milanese means a sauce of tomatoes, mushrooms, grated cheese, shredded meat, and truffles (as opposed to more famous pasta sauces like Alfredo, Bolognese, and Marinara).

Milanesa, used mostly in the Spanish-speaking world but named after Milano, refers to a thin slice of beef, veal, chicken, sometimes pork, possibly eggplant or soy, dipped into beaten eggs, seasoned with salt and garlic or parsley, etc., then rolled in bread crumbs or flour and shallow-fried in oil, a slice at a time. Not dissimilar to Wienerschnitzel!

Sal Mineo was one of the youngest-ever nominees when he was up for a Best Supporting Actor Oscar for *Rebel Without a Cause* (1955). The charismatic Salvatore (born in 1939) got to Hollywood via Broadway after his mother enrolled him in dancing school. He declined to change his name to Sal Miller or Maynard and earned a second nomination for *Exodus* (1960). By the late '60s the ex-teen-idol was reduced to TV roles and returned to the theatre. During rehearsals for a play in Los Angeles in 1976, he was stabbed to death by a robber with a long list of convictions who was nonetheless on the streets.

Minestrone. There is no set recipe for Minestrone, which varies widely from region to region and season to season. It's basically a thick vegetable soup with pasta or rice and often beans, carrots, onions, celery, stock, and tomatoes. It sometimes includes broad beans, lentils, cabbage, mushrooms, asparagus, and turnips. In Italian, minestrare means to serve and minestra is a word for soup.

Minestrone was an ancient Roman staple—minus, of course, the tomatoes—for the empire-builders often had Spartan habits and believed in the healthy benefits of a "frugal" diet, from the Latin word *fruges*, given to vegetables, legumes, and cereals.

Modigliani. As with Dutch painter Vincent Van Gogh, Amedeo Modigliani (1884-1920) enjoyed neither critical nor commercial success in his lifetime. A native of Livorno, the handsome but tubercular Modigliani was a Jewish Italian whose avant-garde portraits were often strikingly elongated, with almond-shaped eyes and linear noses. An independent, he didn't seek easy success by allying with the Cubists or Futurists or imitating Picasso or Marinetti. His style—also in sculpture and poetry—was singular.

In 1906 Amedeo settled in Paris, where he would die in his thirties, like the painters Giorgione and Raphael. Promiscuous and self-destructive, he was addicted to ether, absinthe, and hashish.

In 2003 Modigliani's *Nude Reclining on Her Left Side* (1917) sold for $26.9 million. A year later his 1919 *Jeanne Hebuterne Seated in Front of a Door* sold for $31.3 million. And so it goes.

Fernanda Momigliano (1889-1992), a bestselling cookery writer in 1930s Milan, was described as "a middle-aged Jewish intellectual living with her ailing mother." Her 1933 book *Living Well in Difficult Times: How Women Face Up to the Economic Crisis* offered useful tips to help Italian housewives cope with the aftermath of the 1929 Wall Street Crash and the tightening economic sanctions imposed against Mussolini's Italy by the United Nations. Momigliano's 1936 follow-up book included 16 Jewish recipes (many well known in northern Italy), which took guts on the part of the patriotic school teacher, whose brother was ancient historian Arnaldo Momigliano.

Mona Lisa was born Lisa Gherardini and married a Florentine merchant surnamed del Giocondo, ergo the alternate title of the world's most famous painting, *La Gioconda.* (Mona is a contraction of Madonna, My Lady.) Leonardo's portrait set the style for centuries of portraits to come. His depiction transcended the subject's individuality, representing the eternal feminine of whom it was said, "She is older than the rocks among which she sits." The background is in fact distant, almost a dream landscape. The portrait gives little or no impression of getting to know the subject. The woman's ambiguous expression and her self-contained pose resist familiarity.

Womenswear in la Gioconda's time was tight-fitting, yet Leonardo painted her in a shift, loosely pleated at the neck. In his posthumously published *Treatise on Painting* he urged, "As far as possible avoid the costumes of your own day…so that we may be spared being laughed at by our successors for the mad fashions of men, and leave behind only things that may be admired for their dignity and beauty."

Yves Montand (1921-1991) was born Ivo Livi in Monsummano Terme but at age two his parents fled Italy because of Fascism and moved to Marseilles, France, where by 18 he was singing in music halls but augmenting that meager income as a longshoreman. Then he was discovered by Edith Piaf, who employed him on stage and gave him his start in movies in 1945. He went on to become a French icon of song and film, though his Hollywood career was spotty despite costarring with such big names as Marilyn Monroe and Barbra Streisand. He remained married to Oscar-winner Simone Signoret until her death.

Maria Montessori (1870-1952) was one of the foremost educators of the twentieth century. Born near Ancona, she trained as a medical doctor but became a child psychiatrist and childhood educationalist who researched the most effective early childhood educational methods. She also ran her own school. In 1910 she published *The Montessori Method*, which advocated more individualistic learning, trial-and-error instruction, and self-correction. Her second book, *The Secret of Childhood*, in 1936, focused on child psychology and was also internationally influential. Today, most Western cities have schools that teach Montessori's methods.

Alberto Moravia (1907-1990) was one of Italy's most successful twentieth-century writers—some say the most successful. Nearly all his novels remain in print and are available in English. Many were filmed by major directors with stars like Sophia Loren, Bette Davis, and Brigitte Bardot. A journalist, novelist, playwright, and film critic as well as a political activist, Moravia is perhaps best known for his 1929 debut novel *Gli Indifferenti* (*The Time of Indifference*) and for anti-Fascist novels like *The Conformist* (filmed by Bernardo Bertolucci).

His father was Jewish, his mother Catholic. Anti-Fascist relatives on his father's side were murdered by Mussolini's order, while his maternal uncle was undersecretary of the National Fascist Party. From 1959 to 1962 Moravia was president of the worldwide writers' group PEN International. In 1984 he was elected to the European Parliament as a member of the Italian Communist Party. He once declared, "It is what we are forced to do that forms our character, not what we do of our own free will."

The Morellian Technique. Art critic Giovanni Morelli (1816-1891) came up with a supposedly foolproof way of identifying the authorship of a painting by focusing on its hands, ears, or other "minor" details (hands are central to the Mona Lisa). According to Morelli, this enabled one to look into an artist's subconscious and discover hidden clues. Nobody outside Italy might have heard about this if the technique hadn't been mentioned by Arthur Conan Doyle via Sherlock Holmes and in the work of Sigmund Freud.

Mortadella is the most famous Bolognese pork sausage. A large sausage or cold cut, it's usually sliced thin. A minimum 15 percent of the finely chopped or ground heat-cured pork comprises small cubes of pork fat. Mortadella is traditionally flavored with whole or ground black pepper, myrtle berries, and pistachios.

In the U.S. a commercial version minus the pork fat is known as Bologna sausage, and a variation incorporating olives and pimento is olive loaf.

In the 1971 film *La Mortadella* Sophia Loren isn't allowed to bring a gift mortadella from Italy into the United States. Refusing to give it up, she remains in the New York City Customs office and a diplomatic incident ensues.

Mostaccioli are small southern Italian cakes of flour, honey, orange peel, almonds, and spices. Cut into diamond shapes, after baking they're iced with chocolate. They're also known as mustazzoli and mustazzuoli.

Mostaccioli is also the name of a tubular pasta resembling penne.

Three Mouseketeers. Not long after Disneyland opened, Walt Disney devised *The Mickey Mouse Club*, a 1955 TV series partly designed to lure kids (and their parents) to his theme park. Among the original Mouseketeers was Annette Funicello, age 12. Her mother Virginia Albano's parents had both emigrated from Caserta, near Naples, but only met years later. Annette did several Disney movies, then matured her image but didn't compromise it—keeping her promise to "Uncle Walt" that she would never bare her navel in public—in a series of teenage beach movies with Frankie Avalon (né Avallone) before retiring for several years to raise a family.

Sherry Allen joined the show's cast during its second season at age nine. In the '60s she acted under her original name, Sherry Alberoni, on such TV series as *My Three Sons*, *The Monkees*, *A Family Affair*, and *The Man From U.N.C.L.E.* She subsequently did voice work for animated series like *Josie and the Pussycats*, *Super Friends*, and *The Mighty Orbots*.

In 1957 Don Agrati joined the mouse club at age 13. Later, as Don Grady he costarred for 11 years on the hit sitcom *My Three Sons* as Robbie Douglas. On the shy side, he avoided becoming a teen idol despite his looks, and following the series switched to music, playing with bands and composing for TV, movies, and stage shows. He released a solo jazz album, *Boomer*, in 2008.

Mozzarella is a soft cheese delicious on its own or with fresh bread or of course on pizza. It melts beautifully because it's a pasta filata cheese, made by stretching the curds into strands before molding them. Originally, mozzarella was made in the South, from buffalo's milk. When the Nazis retreated from Italy in World War II, they killed almost all the herds, so now mozzarella is usually made from cow's milk, in the South as well as the North.

The name comes from the verb mozzare: the way handfuls of cheese are ripped away and twisted during the process (from the Latin *mutilis*, to mutilate).

Mr. Coffee. Italians and Italian Americans have long dominated the history of coffee. A particularly successful variation on the filter-drip coffeemaker was invented by Vincent Marotta, the son of immigrants. Marotta played football with the Cleveland Browns before starting a successful construction business in Cleveland. Decades later the dedicated coffee drinker sought to improve the way coffee was made at home. With the help of engineers Edward Able and Erwin Schulze, Marotta developed the Mr. Coffee machine in 1971. Its speed and convenience made it instantly popular and eventually the world's bestselling coffeemaker for domestic use. For decades Mr. Coffee's pitchman was former baseball player (and ex-husband of Marilyn Monroe) Joe DiMaggio.

Naples, aka bella Napoli. It's long been said, "See Naples and die. See Rome and live." The sight of the Bay of Naples and Mt. Vesuvius is breathtaking. Naples retains an impoverished, less orderly image than Rome and more northerly cities, but its regal past has bequeathed it no shortage of incredible palaces, churches, monuments, and museums. Naples is also the birthplace of much of the best of Italian cooking, including pizza and lasagna.

Plus it's the gateway to the splendid Amalfi coast, the awesome ruins of Paestum, Pompeii, and Herculaneum, and the magical islands of Capri and Ischia. And if Naples is less affluent than, say, Florence or Venice, it's also cheaper to visit.

Napoleon. In the 1500s his high-born ancestors moved from the mainland to Corsica. His Italian name was Napoleone di Buonaparte, his Corsican name Napulione or Nabulione Buonaparte. Yes, Napoleon Bonaparte (1769-1821) was a dictator—as were almost all national leaders—and worse, a nakedly ambitious conqueror.

But the emperor of France had some good points. He instituted freedom of religion, even while re-establishing the pre-Revolution primacy of the Catholic Church (privately he confessed that religion was necessary so the masses of poor people wouldn't kill the few rich ones). He mandated that government jobs go to the most qualified, not to the best connected (even while placing all his siblings upon thrones or marrying them to thrones). And he abolished feudalism and created the Napoleonic Code, a more liberal legal code that introduced numerous civil reforms and is still in use in many countries.

> Under the Napoleonic Code, which applies in France and Italy, a citizen's sexual and affectional orientation is not the business of the state. E.M. Forster, who set part of *A Room With a View*, among other novels, in Italy, said he would consider moving there "if the plumbing were only better." Comparing Italy and France with Britain, a character in Forster's *Maurice* (completed in 1914, published in 1971) wonders if same-sex love will ever be accepted in the UK. The other character answers, "I doubt it. England has always been disinclined to accept human nature." That's legally changed, but James Ivory, who directed the films *A Room With a View* and *Maurice*, felt, "The Mediterranean attitude is older as well as more realistic and practical."

Silvio Narizzano's first feature film as a director was *Fanatic* (1965; *Die, Die, My Darling!* in the USA). It was Tallulah Bankhead's last movie; she played a religious fanatic. The next year, the Italian Canadian born in Montreal (1927-2011) helmed his biggest hit, *Georgy Girl*, which earned Lynn Redgrave an Oscar nomination. Narizzano had moved to the UK in the mid 1950s and become a TV director—and later ended his career directing TV in 1995. His other movies included *Loot* (from Joe Orton's play), *Choices* (Demi Moore's screen bow), and *The Class of Miss MacMichael* (starring a pre-Member of Parliament Glenda Jackson). Prone to depression, Narizzano eventually became a semi-recluse obsessed with religious studies.

Neorealism. With the end of the Fascist dictatorship and the return of artistic freedom, Italian filmmakers at the end of WWII adopted a new, less formal, more realistic and populist moviemaking style: neorealism. A picture could focus on ordinary individuals in everyday settings, depicting poverty and life's struggles and injustices without imposing an often-artificial happy ending. Many in Hollywood admired neorealism, but few thought it could make money there. Superstar Ingrid Bergman, who'd come to Hollywood from Sweden, was one of a handful or less who became involved with the new wave of what she called "movies about people and lives, not characters and fantasies."

Franco Nero (born Sparanero in 1941) has played everyone from Sir Lancelot, Gianni Versace, and an author named "Mario Puzzo" (sic) to Claudio Toscanini, father of *Young Toscanini*. His superb looks got him cast in the Hollywood musical *Camelot* (1967), after the flop of which Franco worked primarily in Europe. An affair with *Camelot* costar Vanessa Redgrave produced a son (writer-director Carlo, born in 1969) but no marriage—a scandal at the time. Redgrave and Nero did tie the knot in 2006. Franco has continued in big and little roles in over 150 movies, including several spaghetti westerns, and received a star on the Italian Walk of Fame in Toronto in 2011.

The North of Italy has been more prosperous and business-oriented than the South as long as people can remember. Director Luchino Visconti, from Milan, proudly acknowledged having Teutonic ancestors. "Remember that in the 6th century Italy was invaded by the Lombards, a Germanic people. In what is now called Lombardy, certainly, they left a lasting impression of what one must admit is a greater efficiency and regard for education and industry than one finds farther south."

Northern wine tours and tasting. Ever since the ancient Greeks introduced their *passito* technique (using partially dried grapes) to northern Italy, the region has excelled in wine production. The scenic (and bicycle-friendly) area offers umpteen kilometers for wine tours and tastings. From Valpolicella's reds, Amarone and Recioto, and the whites of Soave to Oltrepo Pavese in the east to Leonardo's preferred Valtellina in the Alpine foothills and the fizz of Franciacorte in Brescia, the North is an oenophile's paradise.

(Call ahead to verify that a given winery is open at a given time.)

Not Italian, but we like 'em anyway. "Some people say I have this sensual quality that ties in with being Italian, but I'm not," said Marlon Brando, who won a second Academy Award as Vito Corleone in *The Godfather*. Depending on the source, "Brando" was originally French (Brandeu) or German (Brandau, later Brandow).

As for Henry Fonda (and Jane and Peter and Bridget), the name was said to originate with an Italian who immigrated to Holland in the 1400s or 1500s, but it hasn't been genealogically proven. However, one of Henry's wives was an Italian baroness.

Among the *Wizard of Oz* Munchkins, Ruth Duccini (the last surviving female Munchkin) and Margaret Pellegrini were not Italian—their husbands were.

Novella. When there's not enough time to read an entire novel or it's not that interesting, a novella comes in handy. It's a short novel or a long short story; a famous example is Truman Capote's *Breakfast at Tiffany's*. We call it a novella—the feminine of novello, meaning new—because it was a new genre of literature begun in the early Renaissance, especially the 1300s and particularly via Boccaccio's *Decameron* (see earlier entry).

Capote, sometimes mistaken for Italian due to his surname—his Cuban stepfather's—once said, "I assume if we'd been Italian my parents would have paid more attention to me."

Nutella. How popular is this chocolate spread that's Europe's kiddie equivalent of peanut butter? The company that makes it uses one-fourth of the world's supply of hazelnuts. Nutella was created in the 1940s by Pietro Ferrero, a baker from Alba, Piedmont, an area known for hazelnuts. The product was originally a solid block. In 1951 Ferrero began producing a creamy version, Supercrema. In 1964 the renamed Nutella went Europe-wide and was an instant success.

Also cherished are cocoa solids, and skimmed milk. In the U.S. Nutella contains soy products, and February 5 is World Nutella Day.

Olive oil didn't begin in Italy, and olive trees, which have been cultivated there since 600 BCE, were likely introduced by the Greeks, who'd already been growing olives for a few millennia. But Italian cuisine's varied use of olive oil is unrivaled and a key component of the healthier Mediterranean diet. Most of Italy's olives are grown in the South and on the islands of Sicily and Sardinia, accounting for some 20 percent of global output. Almost all Italian olives are processed into olive oil.

The liquid's healthful properties are said to extend to the complexion. According to actress Anna Magnani, "For good skin, olive oil! Inside you and on you."

"O Sole Mio" means Oh, My Sun. What other country has a love song to the sun, celebrating in beautiful melody and joyous lyrics the taken-for-granted but indispensable star of which our planet is a lucky satellite? The Neapolitan song was composed in 1898 by Eduardo di Capua and Giovanni Capurro.

The sunny standard has been recorded by hundreds of singers, from Caruso and Rosa Ponselle to Tony Bennett (*né* Benedetto) and Piccola Pupa. In 1980 Luciano Pavarotti's rendition earned a Grammy for Best Classical Vocal Performance. Elvis Presley's totally re-worded English version, "It's Now or Never," became an international hit.

At the 1920 Olympics in Antwerp, Belgium, "O Sole Mio" was played when nobody could locate the music to the Italian national anthem. Today the tune announces the happy approach of ice cream vans throughout Europe.

Ossobuco means bone with a hole and is a specialty of Milan. The milk-fed veal shanks are prized for their tasty bone marrow and are slowly braised with vegetables in a combination of broth and white wine until the tenderized meat falls off the bone. Ossobuco is traditionally served with risotto alla Milanese. The modern version includes tomatoes. The original doesn't, and is flavored with cinnamon, bay leaf, and gremolata, a chopped herb condiment of lemon zest, parsley, and garlic.

Other cheeses. Besides internationally famous ones like Parmigiano, Mozzarella, Provolone, Ricotta, and Gorgonzola, Italy has hundreds of regional and local cheeses. Among them:

Bagoss—a mature, strong-flavored, and grainy grating cheese from Lombardy.

Caciocavallo—a historic Sicilian cow's milk cheese similar to Provolone.

Caprino—Italian goat cheese.

Manteca—cheese with a butter center from Basilicata.

Marzolino—a historic sheep's cheese, made near Siena and Florence.

Robiola—a soft-ripened cheese with a thin rind from Piedmont of cow's milk, sometimes blended with sheep's or goat's milk.

Taleggio—an aromatic, flavorful soft cheese from Lombardy made with cow's milk.

Al Pacino. Believe it or not, Alfredo Pacino (born 1940) started out as a stand-up comic. Though he grew up on the movies his Italian American mother took him to, he came late to motion pictures, debuting in 1969 but soon finding stardom as Michael Corleone in *The Godfather* saga. He also starred as *Serpico* (1974), the story of real-life cop Frank Serpico, and *Donnie Brasco* (1997). Pacino won an Oscar for *Scent of a Woman* (1992), a remake of the 1974 Italian movie *Profumo di Donna*.

Niccolo Paganini is possibly the greatest-ever composer and performer of violin music. Born in Genoa (1782-1840), he was taken to Parma at age 12 by his father to learn whether a celebrated teacher and composer would take his son as a student. While waiting, Niccolo began to play a concert from sheet music left on a desk. The maestro rushed into the room and declared, "I have nothing to teach you. You are wasting your time here."

At 23 the handsome Pagnanini became Lucca's opera director. Four years later he began traveling the continent, performing his own music so brilliantly and successfully that a rumor spread that he'd "sold his soul to the devil." Relocated to Paris, Paganini inspired Chopin, Liszt, and others, and afforded fiscal aid to aspiring composers like Hector Berlioz. When he died, Paganini was refused burial in a cemetery because Church officials believed the devil-rumor. So his body lay in a casket in a cellar in Nice, and wasn't buried in Italy until 56 years after his death.

Palermo's Capuchin catacombs. From Rome to Lima, Peru, many cities feature catacombs that draw some visitors and repel others. One of the more interesting is under the Church of the Capuchins in Palermo, Sicily. About four centuries ago it was discovered that the air in church and monastery cellars could mummify cadavers. Such cellars became popular resting places for rich and (mostly) poor alike, typically dressed in their best clothes. Between 1599 and 1920 about 8,000 bodies filled the Capuchins' Gallery of the Dead, with relatives visiting their dead and rewiring those corpses which had collapsed and replacing the clothes that had disintegrated.

The last body placed in the gallery was two-year-old Rosalia Lombardo, nicknamed the Little Sleeping Beauty because her glass-encased remains are still so lifelike.

Buried in the church's cemetery is Sicilian Giuseppe Tomasi di Lampedusa, the prince who wrote the novel *The Leopard*, classically filmed by Luchino Visconti.

Andrea Palladio is the only architect (1508-1580) whose name applies to a still-extant style of architecture, Palladian. Born near Vicenza, he worked mostly in and around that city—about halfway between Verona and Padua. Originally a stonemason, he designed public buildings, a theatre, palaces, and country villas. Of the latter, one of the most famous was the Villa Rotonda di Valmarana, which influenced Thomas Jefferson's design for his own Monticello as well as the Rotunda of the University of Virginia (the Italian villa's most recent owner, Mario Valmarana, was a professor of architecture at the University of Virginia).

Palladio eventually set down the influential principles by which he'd designed and built in *The Four Books of Architecture*.

Panettone, whose root is the word for bread, was once a northern Italian specialty. Now it's a national Christmas-time treat, served in the morning with coffee or in the evening with a sweet wine. The tall, aromatic, raisin- and candied-fruit-studded bread is a more delicious and appreciated gift equivalent of the Anglo fruitcake. Leftover panettone is tasty toasted and spread with butter or mascarpone cheese or combined with other ingredients to make Panettone Bread Pudding. Mangia!

The Pantheon. For some 1,800 years this temple in Rome to all their gods boasted the biggest true dome—a halved geometric sphere—in the world. Instigated and possibly designed by the emperor Hadrian (76-138 CE), it came too late for inclusion in the list of seven wonders of the ancient Greek world. For centuries upon centuries, rulers exhorted their architects to match or exceed the Pantheon. All failed, and only modern technology and material sciences have enabled the construction of larger domes. Even so, it remains the largest unreinforced concrete dome on earth. This amazing and beautifully surviving (despite earthquakes and the elements) edifice more than merits visiting and reading about.

Parma, in the heartland of Emilia-Romagna, is renowned for good food and easy living. It offers the visitor many sights, including excellent medieval buildings, a major opera house, and outstanding paintings and sculpture. But more than its lifestyle or any individual building or artwork, Parma is famed for its cheese, its ham, and its violets.

Parma ham and prosciutto crudo. The former is made, as it has been for centuries, from pigs fattened on whey left over from the making of Parmigiano, or Parmesan cheese. Distinctively flavored, it is cured in the breezy hills south of Parma, and aged up to ten months. It's eaten uncooked and thinly sliced, as is prosciutto crudo, or raw cured ham, which also includes salt and pepper. Each Parma ham is branded with the former duchy of Parma's five-pointed crown.

Parma violets were first found in Italy in the 1500s and descend from an exotic branch of that plant family. Their lavender flowers vary in size. The purple flower of a smaller, more delicate Parma violet is transformed into a violet-scented crystallized sweet named Parma Violets made since the 1930s by Swizzels Matlow, a UK confectionary manufacturer. They're often used to decorate food, usually desserts.

Parmesan cheese, or Parmigiano, is one of the best known in the world and is central to Italian cuisine. In the thirteenth and fourteenth centuries, certain cities in northern Italy gave their names to cheeses that made them famous and prosperous, e.g., Parmigiano (which still refers to any person or thing related to Parma), Piacentino, and Lodigiano. These became a must for those who could afford them, typically as a condiment for pasta, along with butter and some "sweet spice," usually cinnamon—remember that tomato sauce was unknown until Europe "discovered" Mexico.

There are two varieties of Parmesan: A-class Parmigiano-Reggiano (aged for about 18 months) and B-class Grana. The cheese is still made—for seven centuries—with partially skimmed milk added to whey to create fermentation, with rennet to curdle the milk. Then the cheese is salted and shaped. Though used primarily in grated form, it's delicious in cooking or eaten solo or with pears—an Italian specialty.

Pier Paolo Pasolini (1922-1975) was a poet, novelist, critic, *provocateur*, and an acclaimed, often banned director of varied movies. Early on, he focused on female and male prostitution and Italian shantytowns. Later subjects ranged from religion, to urban polysexuality (*Teorema*) to The Canterbury Tales (including a gay love scene that shocked in 1972) to classical Greece in *Medea* (1969). Pasolini's last movie, *Salo* (1975), was deliberately scandalous and grotesque, to mirror Salo, the final Fascist republic set up in 1943 as the government fled north to escape the Allied invasion. Soon after the highly controversial *Salo*'s release, the gay filmmaker's mutilated body was discovered upon rough terrain near Ostia.

Pasta literally means paste, and neither Marco Polo nor anyone else introduced it to Italy from China. The ancient Romans were eating pasta before they knew there was a China. "Pasta" pertains to any sort of dough or foods made from dough, e.g., noodles, dumplings, and pastries.

Surprisingly, pasta was consumed primarily by the more affluent until the Industrial

Revolution made flour for pasta more affordable for the working classes in the late 1800s. Pasta became more widespread during the economic boom following World War II. Before that, some 80 percent of rural Italians ate a plant-based diet, with pasta reserved for feast days, usually in a legume soup.

> Italians eat over 60 pounds of pasta per person a year, about twice what Americans do (paradoxically, there's less obesity in Italy). Did you know that before mechanization pasta was made in a large trough and kneaded by foot? Or that saying "una pasta" (a pasta) changes the meaning to a store-bought pastry? References to stuffed pasta like ravioli go back to at least the 1300s, at which time most (non-stuffed) forms of pasta were called vermicelli (little worms). In the 1700s that term was basically replaced by maccheroni (sic), and Naples, which boasted 280 pasta shops in 1785, was the capital of pasta-making.
>
> Italian pasta comes in two versions: pasta fresca is freshly made and from soft wheat, while pasta secca is dried pasta, typically commercially made. By law it can only be made with hard semola di grano duro wheat flour.

> Is there no end to the shapes of Italian pasta? Categories include pasta lunga —long circular, hollow, or ribboned strips or ribbons such as spaghetti, spaghettini, linguine, fettucine, tagliatelle, capellini, etc., in numbered grades.
>
> Pasta corta—short, whether tubes or cylinders, smooth or ridged, like maccheroni (macaroni), penne, rigatoni, fusilli, etc., also shapes like gigli (lilies) and denti d'elefante (elephant's teeth), etc., and openwork patterns like rotelli (wheels), etc.
>
> Pasta stampata tipo Bologna are Bologna-type pressed and twisted shapes, like farfalle (square, nipped in the center to resemble a butterfly) and cravattine (bow ties), etc.
>
> Pastina are miniscule and meant for soup, often resembling grains or seeds or even trout's eyes (occhi di trota). Et cetera!

Luciano Pavarotti, known as the king of tenors, was possibly the most popular tenor since Caruso. (And, unlike for instance Franco Corelli or singer-actor Mario Lanza, one of the more likeable.) Pavarotti's voice was big, beautiful, and pleasing, as was his desire to please. However, in a quest for greater popularity he sometimes undertook roles that revealed a limited versatility. Primarily self-taught, he frequently overstretched his ability, and his one Hollywood vehicle (*Yes, Giorgio*, 1982) failed. But Pavarotti, who was born and died in Modena (1935-2007), sang successfully throughout the world and repopularized operatic classical singing in a big way.

Pecorino means little sheep and is a hard sharp cheese made from fresh ewe's milk. Romano is the most famous regional variation—sometimes simply called Romano cheese. It's described in the *De Rustica* of Lucius Junius Moderatus Columella, who stopped in Rome in the first century BCE, having reached Italy with Hannibal's troops. Romano is always aged, about eight months. Pecorino Senese's rind is rubbed with tomato paste. Sicilian pecorinos often feature black peppercorns.

Nancy Pelosi became the United States' first female Speaker of the House in 2007. The Democrat, born in 1940 and a mother of five, had served 20 years in Congress. After being sworn in, she stated, "For our daughters and our granddaughters today, we have broken the marble ceiling. For our daughters and our granddaughters, now the sky is the limit." On the day she gaveled the House to order, she urged, "We have made history, now let us make progress."

Peperoni, or sweet peppers, arrived in Italy shortly after their discovery in the Americas. However, for about two centuries, peppers—sweet or hot—were deemed poor people's food and weren't found in Italian culinary encyclopedias until the 1800s. Peppers are classified by shape in Italy: peperoni a corno (horn-shaped) are elongated, whether curved or straight; peperoni a cuore di bue (ox's heart) are heart-shaped; peperoni a pomodoro (tomato-shaped) are compressed and small; and peperoni quadrati (four-sided) are boxy.

Pepperoni is a beef and pork sausage seasoned with peperone—plural: peperoni, sweet peppers or chilis. Thus the name refers to one seasoning ingredient rather than the sausage itself, whose cured meats are usually mashed together. By any other name, it's heaven-on-a-cheese-and-tomato-sauce-topped crust…that is, pepperoni pizza.

In Italian pepperoni is usually called salsiccia Napoletana piccante, spicy Neapolitan sausage.

Perspective. Imagine paintings without perspective. Imagine forgetting about perspective. Yet that's what happened. The vanishing point, basis of the theory of linear perspective, was known to the Greeks and Romans but was forgotten by the Dark Ages. It was reintroduced by Florentine architect-engineers Filippo Brunelleschi (1377-1446) and Leon Battista Alberti (1404-1472). In his highly influential *Della Pintura* (*On Painting*, 1436) Alberti codified the principles of realistic painting.

The principles, lost for so long, were applied by Masaccio (1401-1428), sometimes called the father of Renaissance painting and a friend of Brunelleschi. An artistic revolution ensued. In addition, cartographers experimented with perspective and the "point at infinity" whereat parallel lines appear to converge, the better to make more accurate maps of the world.

Pesto, pounded with a pestle and mortar, refers to any sauce made with mashed ingredients. The best known is Genoa's basil pesto, made from basil, garlic, and pine nuts pounded in olive oil. Other typical ingredients include aromatic herbs, garlic, salt, and Parmigiano and/or Fiore Sardo (cheese made of sheep's milk). The mixture may be moistened with vinegar, broth, or verjuice—sour juice, usually from unripe grapes or crab apples.

Simple and subtle yet flavorful, pesto is frequently used on pasta. The ancient Roman version, moretum, was made of garlic, cheese, and herbs. Pesto didn't become widely popular in North America until the 1980s and '90s.

Piano. The piano—short for its full name, pianoforte, meaning softly/loudly—was invented in 1709 by Bartolomeo Cristofori, an instrument maker who deserves to be more famous than he is. Over the next century, the piano was continuously developed until its levers' action was just so and the instrument could play softly or loudly. This enabled a melody to stand out from the quieter accompaniment and it meant a player could vary the loudness and timbre of a piece in order to emphasize its emotional climaxes. A piano is about the only instrument which, solo, can pleasingly perform any type of music, from pop to classical to ragtime to a lullaby.

Piccola Pupa means Little Doll. The singer-actress (born Giuliana Crimilde Coverlizza, year unknown) was discovered for U.S. television, and in 1963 and '64 appeared on four episodes of the sitcom *Make Room for Daddy*. Billed as "Little Miss Dynamite," the juvenile was a guest on *The Ed Sullivan Show* in 1964, singing "Quando, Quando, Quando" and "Stessa Spiaggia, Stessa Mare," and did other shows as well. She acted in a few beach movies, including *The Ghost in the Invisible Bikini* in 1966, before choosing to quit show business. Now a mother of two and a grandmother, she lives in Rapallo on the Italian Riviera.

Piccola means little but is also the English name of a half-size flute—ottavino in Italian—featuring most of the same fingerings as a standard flute but playing an octave higher than written. In orchestras, piccolos frequently play together with violins or flutes, to add contrast and piquancy to the melody.

"Piccolo" was first used instrumentally in the U.S. around 1854, about a dozen years after its bow in Britain.

Pininfarina. Those who revere cars esteem the prestigious automobile design firm and coach builder founded in 1930 in Cambiano by Battista "Pinin" Farina. Over the decades it has designed not only Italian vehicles but for General Motors, Peugeot, etc., and now for Chinese auto manufacturers.

Pininfarina also designs yachts, private jets and airplanes, people movers, buses, trams, high-speed trains, automated light-rail cars, and rolling stocks.

Via a subsidiary, the firm consults on interior, graphic, and industrial design and on architecture. Battista's son Sergio confessed, "It is a mystery why we design so well in art, clothing, and machines, but Italians love beauty and have the talent. We take the time…beauty is not fast, it is not assembly-line."

Pinocchio's nose, as most every child knows, grows longer when he lies. *The Adventures of Pinocchio* was published in 1883 by Carlo Lorenzini, who took the surname Collodi. The children's classic told of a woodcarver named Gepetto who much wants a son, and the temptations and tribulations of a puppet made of pinewood who much wants to become a real boy. The Disney animated-movie version in 1940 much expanded the Italian tale's popularity.

Luigi Pirandello is best known as the playwright of *Six Characters in Search of an Author* (1921) and *Henry IV* (1922). He won a Nobel Prize for his work, which numbered 56 plays—12 in his Sicilian dialect and 44 in Italian—246 short stories, and lots of literary criticism. A gentle soul whose work reflected his pessimism, he taught in Rome and tended his mentally ill wife and their three children until she attempted to fatally stab him while he slept.

The Pirelli Building, a 32-storey grattaciello—skyscraper—was nicknamed Pirellone (Big Pirelli). For many years it was Italy's tallest structure as well as a symbol of Milan and of Italy's economic boom. Designed by Gio Ponti with Pier Luigi Nervi and Arturo Danusso assisting, in 1958 it was one of the first such constructions to eschew the typical block form. Rather, its classic lines and tapered sides were internationally admired, and it inspired the '60s Pan Am Building in Manhattan (now the MetLife Building). It was erected on the site of Pirelli's first factory in the 1800s.

In 1971 Pirelli merged equitably with Britain's Dunlop tire company. It was regarded as a harbinger for inter-European business growth, but Dunlop-Pirelli unmerged in 1981.

Pisa. Besides Venice, Genoa, and Amalfi, Pisa was one of Italy's four principal seafaring republics and a significant maritime power whose highpoint was the 1100s. Today it's about ten miles from the Mediterranean, due to accumulation of organic matter via the Arno River. Back then, Pisa had a powerful navy to protect the profitable trading interests that helped finance its magnificent public and religious buildings. The decline of Pisa began in the mid and late 1200s, when it was defeated by Florence and then Genoa—the latter loss cost 5,000 Pisan lives, and 11,000 were taken prisoner.

Pizza. Definitions often fail to convey an item's psychological, visual, olfactory, and gustatory appeal. For instance, pizza: "Flat yeast bread topped with a wide variety of ingredients, but principally tomato, mozzarella, and basil," per *The Dictionary of Italian Food and Drink*. Pizza, which began in Naples, was surprisingly little known even in northern Italy, let alone outside the country, until after World War II. Today some 62 million Italians consume over three billion pizzas annually—typically served as an individual pie for one or as a square slice cut from a whole.

Pizza is now universal, not only a primo comfort food, an ideal takeaway food, and a convenient order-in food, but perhaps the world's favorite food, period.

Its first recorded mention was in 997 CE in Gaeta, southern Italy. The words pizzo and pizza mean edge or point and the verb pizzicare means to pinch or, musically, to pluck.

Polenta is a commonplace fixture of Italian cooking, by way of maize flour. But since corn was unknown until the sixteenth-century conquest of Mexico, polenta—from Latin, "pearl barley"—originally referred to any pulse or grain boiled to mush or porridge and flavored with cheese, herbs, bacon, etc. Cooked cornmeal became a mainstay of poor people's diet for centuries.

Today polenta is a comfort food, for instance baked polenta layered with melting cheese or with butter and Parmesan or mushrooms fried with garlic or bits of cooked sausage, etc., a happy meal with a requisite green salad.

Pompeii and Herculaneum but also the towns of Stabiae and Oplontis were destroyed by the volcanic eruption of Mt. Vesuvius at dawn on August 24, 79 CE. Pompeii, covering 158 acres, had the most inhabitants, about 20,000. Hot lava, gases, pumice rocks, mud, and ashes buried the towns and also preserved them for posterity, giving interested visitors almost two millennia later a unique view of how Italians once lived.

Visible at one Herculaneum bakery are carbonized bread, cookies, and pizza—probably the oldest known pizza, though lacking tomato sauce, for Europe hadn't yet imported the tomato.

Vesuvius, which broods over the city and bay of Naples, last erupted in March 1944.

The Poodle Cut. The story goes that in the 1950s an aristocratic Frenchwoman gave a party and had her hairdresser cut and style her poodle's hair into a chic bob with bangs (called fringe in England). The pooch was the hit of the party, inspiring the hostess to have her hair done the same way. The boyish bob spread through France and Italy—Gina Lollobridgida was one of the first stars to wear it—then arrived in the U.S. The most famous example of the poodle cut was probably Audrey Hepburn in *Roman Holiday* (1953), in which the princess's traditional long hair is cheerfully shorn by an Italian coiffeur into the perky, more fashionable 'do.

The Poor House of Naples (L'Albergo dei Poveri) was planned by Charles III—the first Bourbon monarch of the Kingdom of Naples—in 1751 to house the city's poor and homeless and teach them a trade. Architect Ferdinando Fuga designed the five-story edifice with a façade some 1,100 feet (335.3 meters) long, incorporating five internal courtyards and a huge, high-domed central church. Construction continued until 1829, when the original plans were shelved. At one time it housed 5,000 people. Uncompleted, it remains one of the biggest buildings in the world and has variously been used for trade schools, city archives, hospitals, soccer fields, exhibition sites, concerts, and private functions. In 2006 the imposing structure's façade was restored.

Prada, a Milan store selling suitcases and leather goods, opened in 1913 but really took off when Mario Prada's granddaughter Miuccia assumed the reins in 1978. In the 1980s she added a ready-to-wear clothing line and in the '90s high-fashion accessories. At one time a mime actress, Miuccia Prada holds a doctorate in political science but excels in business and marketing. Hollywood clients helped put Prada on the international map, and today Prada boasts boutiques in major cities around the world.

The 2006 movie *The Devil Wears Prada*, based on Lauren Weisberger's bestselling *roman à clef*, features Meryl Streep as a boss from hell who never—ever—raises her voice.

Prego sauce isn't really Italian—it was "introduced" in 1981 by the Campbell Soup Company, its recipe created by one of their cooks. But it tastes good and it usually accompanies Italian food. Prego of course means you're welcome, don't mention it, and please. The sauce comes in over 20 flavors, among them marinara, mini-meatball, zesty mushroom, and roasted garlic Parmesan. Prego also features an organic line.

Paula Prentiss was born Paula Ragusa in Texas in 1938. Tall and gurgle-voiced, the star charmed and amused in *Where the Boys Are*, *What's New, Pussycat? The World* *of Henry Orient*, and others, but in the mid '60s put movies aside to dwell on marriage and motherhood. Her most notable '70s film was the original *Stepford Wives*.

Her sister Ann Prentiss (1939-2010) had a lower-key acting career.

The Prince, written in 1513 and published posthumously in 1532, remains one of the most enduring yet controversial of nonreligious books. This primer on statecraft is still consulted by the ambitious, in or out of politics, and is taught in psychology and poli-sci college classes. The book's image is primarily negative, and its author, Florentine civil servant Niccolo Machiavelli (1469-1527), has often been accused of promoting lying, cheating, and worse. But basically, Machiavelli, whose name has become a nefarious adjective—machiavellian—detailed how a leader acquires and retains influence and power, often a necessarily two-faced undertaking.

"A ruler should act sometimes as a lion, sometimes as a fox," advised Machiavelli, who didn't deny that power corrupts.

Machiavelli also penned a famous Renaissance comedy, *La Mandragola* (*The Mandrake*).

Francesco Procopio, a destitute Palermo aristocrat, immigrated to Vienna in 1672 and worked for a coffee merchant before opening his own coffeehouse. It prospered, a string followed, and in 1675 Procopio moved to Paris and opened the Café Procope (it still exists, in a third location), the first Parisian café that sold ices.

But it was Procopio's custard-based ice cream that sparked a revolution. Soon, coffeehouses all over Paris were selling ice cream. Then Italian coffeehouses based on his French model proliferated and gelato became a national rage in Procopio's homeland.

Pronto. In most languages, one answers the phone with "Hello?" or its equivalent. How blah. Italian doesn't use an insincere greeting to heaven-knows-whom that's voiced with a question mark. Rather, one says, **"Pronto,"** declaring oneself ready to be vocally engaged.

Provolone is one of Italy's signature cheeses, sharp, spicy, and high-scented, from cow's milk, typically with a tough wax rind and originating in southern Italy. There are variations: provolone dolce is considerably milder, made with calf's rennet. Provolone picante is a strong spicy version made with kid's or lamb rennet and aged.

Provolette is small provolone, provole is medium, and provoloni (sic) is large, reaching up to five or six feet. Like mozzarella, provolone is a pasta filata cheese, made by stretching the curds into strands before molding them.

The quattrocento (literally 400) is the 1400s, when Italy bridged the late Middle Ages and early Renaissance, and individualism and dimension became more prominent in the arts and philosophy. For instance, Byzantine mosaics became passé, and the influence of Constantinople, the self-styled Eastern Roman Empire, faded. There was less stained glass, fewer frescoes and illuminated manuscripts, and more sculpture inspired by the classical styles of Greece and Rome. Art generally became more secular and less flat.

Ragu is a meat-based sauce, usually served with pasta. Traditional ragu is a sauce of braised or stewed meat flavored with tomatoes, as opposed to a tomato sauce flavored by the addition of meat. The first known recipe for a meat sauce in which the cooked meat was an integral part of the sauce accompanying pasta is from the late 1700s.

Raphael (1483-1520) is the English name for Raffaello Sanzio, usually considered the third genius painter of the Renaissance, with da Vinci and Michelangelo. A heterosexual, he had the opportunity to indulge his sexual appetites frequently and died at 37. Where Leonardo was slow and pensive—with boundless curiosity—and Michelangelo was soured and temperamental, Raphael was cheerful and made friends and paintings easily (much to Michelangelo's disgust). In his twenties Raphael was hired by the pope to execute frescos in the Vatican palace, alas painting over works by past masters.

Pope Leo X much admired Raphael and would have made him a cardinal had he given up his busy social life. Michelangelo once told Raphael he looked like a "courtesan"—a prostitute. Raphael responded that his elder resembled a "hangman." Raphael's first biographer, Vasari, wrote, "Raphael kept up his secret affairs…with no sense of moderation….He went to excess and returned home afterward with a violent fever" that killed him. The painter is buried in Rome's Pantheon.

Ravioli, little egg-pasta pillows with serrated edges encasing a meat, cheese, vegetable, or fish filling, are found throughout Italy. Depending on the region, the shape may change to more rounded or even triangular, half-moon, or hat-shaped.

The name may also change. Ravioli were first written about in the 1300s, and during the First World War the Italian army pioneered canned ravioli, later popularized in Europe by Buitoni and Heinz and in the U.S. by Chef Boyardee.

The Red Cross was founded by Swiss businessman Henri Dunant, who was horrified to witness the absence of care and facilities for the victims of two 1859 battles in the northern Italian towns of Solferino and San Martino that had to do with the Risorgimento, or unification of Italy. At that time, 135,000 Piedmontese and French soldiers fought 140,000 Austrian soldiers, and 19,000 horses and almost 1,000 cannons were also involved. Some 9,800 men were killed, 20,000 were wounded, and 11,400 went missing or were taken prisoner.

Solferino, in the Lakes district, has a museum dedicated to the battles and a Red Cross monument. An ossuary in its San Pietro church contains the bones of over 7,000 soldiers.

The Renaissance. Interesting that we use a French word, meaning rebirth, to describe this basically Italian movement—the Rinascimento. The dictionary defines it as a revival of art and literature under the influence of classical models during the fourteenth through the sixteenth centuries. It was also an attempt to expand possibilities in art and in life—two steps forward, and one step back, from the strictures of contemporary religion. As historian George Holmes put it, "The civilization of Renaissance Italy had to live, easily or uneasily, with the Christian Church." Pagan and humanist ideas and goals in art and philosophy had to deal with the power structures (church and city-states) of the time. Nonetheless, the Renaissance initiated permanent socio-cultural changes that in time would gain momentum.

> Why did the Renaissance begin in Italy? Factors pointing to the right place at the right time include the ample presence of ancient Roman (and sometimes Greek) ruins, reminders of a great past. Also, Italy's fragmented city-states were not only acquisitive and combative, but highly competitive, seeking to outdo each other on every level. Many city-states, wealthy via trade and conquest, became proud and generous patrons of the arts and fledgling sciences. As Constantinople—seat of the Greek-speaking Eastern Roman Empire—faded and fell (conquered and converted by the Ottoman Turks in 1453), its Christian and Jewish scholars and artists moved west, often to Italy.
>
> The oldest existing book in the world is the Buddhist *Diamond Sutra* from China in 868 CE, but the spread in 1400s Europe of the printing press enabled the diffusion of learning and ideas from ancient Greece, Rome, and elsewhere.

Ribollita. Everyone's heard of minestrone, but Tuscany's most typical and favorite soup is ribollita, a twice-boiled vegetable soup and rustic tradition that includes winter vegetables, day-old bread, and olive oil. Long, slow cooking brings all its flavors fully out. Ingredients vary by season, area, and personal taste, but three are required: one- or two-day old Tuscan bread, white beans, and black kale.

If one visits Florence, almost no trattoria won't list ribollita on its menu.

Ricotta means "re-cooked." It's a by-product of excess whey from cheese-making that morphs into a delicious soft, lumpy cheese from cow's, sheep's, goat's, or Italian water buffalo's milk. Similar to some variants of cottage cheese, it dates back to at least 2,000 BCE in Italy and was eventually consumed by ancient Roman aristocrats as well as medieval shepherds. Emilia-Romagna and Bologna's ricotta is especially sweet and creamy.

Ricotta may be used in entrees or desserts, particularly cheesecake, cannoli, and cookies.

Risotto alla Milanese. Rice, or riso, is northern Italy's staple (pasta was imported from the south in the 1600s). The Po Valley grows about 50 varieties of rice. The nation's rice capital is Pavia, where the signature dish is rice with crispy frogs' legs, called risotto con le rane. Milan's specialty is the world-famous risotto alla Milanese, traditionally simmered in meat broth or marrow stock, wine, butter, and saffron. Buon appetito!

Roads. All roads lead to Rome, the saying goes, and those master builders constructed roads with Roman concrete, building them in quantity and quality throughout their empire for military, trade, and communication purposes, and to bind and Romanize what they deemed their world—they who called the Mediterranean *Mare Nostrum*, Our Sea. Roman roads, like their aqueducts and bridges, still serve in numerous countries.

Simon Rodia's monumental personal creation was the Watts Towers in Los Angeles. In the 1920s the immigrant tile setter from Serino, Avellino (1879-1965), began embedding found objects like tiles, dishes, bottles, cans, and odd pieces of metal into soaring, spiraling concrete, incorporating references to Christopher Columbus and Joan of Arc, etc., and including Native American and Spanish motifs. By the time the curving pinnacles drew notice beyond Rodia's South Central neighborhood in the 1950s, they were nearly complete. The media took notice and people came to look.

In 1959 the Los Angeles Building and Safety Department declared the towers a hazard, stating Rodia had no formal engineering background. The public and media protested, and Rodia's work was tested via a 10,000-pound weight trying to pull the highest tower out of plumb. In 1965 the towers were declared a Cultural-Historical Monument, but the same year, the racially motivated Watts Riots broke out, and for decades most would-be visitors avoided the neighborhood, which today is primarily Hispanic.

Roman Holiday was a rare on-location Hollywood movie in 1953, made in Rome so that Paramount Studios could use up some of their local funds that weren't transferable to the U.S. The story of a stifled princess visiting the Eternal City who escapes her entourage and falls in love before returning to her royal duties made an international star and Oscar

Award Winner of Audrey Hepburn, and showed off Rome beautifully. Local tourism boomed after the picture—now a classic—became a hit.

> Audrey Hepburn returned to Rome to film producer Dino DeLaurentiis's version of Tolstoi's *War and Peace* (1956). She settled in Rome in 1969 when she married psychiatrist Andrea Dotti. As Hepburn's career had far outshone that of first husband Mel Ferrer (an actor-director), she temporarily retired "to become an Italian housewife" and, for the second time, became a mother. She lived in Rome until 1982.

Roman numerals. Okay, they're initially intimidating and can seem cumbersome once they add up. But they're classy and fun to master—and impress your friends with how educated you are. They're often still used after the copyright symbol and for movie sequels. They also lend dignity—or pretentiousness, e.g., Henry Spofford III, instead of Henry Spofford 3.

Rome. The Eternal City. The capital of an empire, later the capital of a religion, a city with possibly more sights to see than any other on earth. But what was it about the inhabitants of this one city in central Italy, a republic before it became a civilization, that caused or enabled them to supersede all other cities on the peninsula, not to mention all others in Europe, and become a world power? Any reader of Roman history recognizes that for all its admirable and impressive qualities, Rome and its culture exhibited grievous flaws, among them arrogance, hypocrisy, imperialism, and vengeance—as in the utter destruction of rival Carthage and entire city-states in Greece.

Still, Rome's accomplishments and enduring legacy are stunning, and the city itself a priceless jewel.

Romeo and Juliet are known in Italy as Juliet and Romeo. Shakespeare's play (ca. 1594) was based on novelist Luigi Da Porto of Vicenza's story, written around 1530. The rival Capulet and Montecchi families did live in Verona a few centuries earlier, but there's no historical evidence for their literarily famous offspring. Even so, visiting the "sites" of Romeo and Juliet is a profitable business in Verona that takes in Romeo's house, Juliet's tomb, and her house, with its romance-laden balcony—added in 1935.

The timeless story's chief value is its poetic representation of self-determination. Even today, when much or most of the world is told whom to marry, the Veronese couple exemplifies, albeit tragically, the maxim "to thine own self be true."

Franco Rossellini (1935-1992) was the son of composer Renzo Rossellini, best known for his film scores, and the nephew of director Roberto Rossellini, for both of whom Franco initially worked. He became an assistant director and sometime actor but made his name as the producer of such '60s and '70s movies as Pasolini's *Teorema*, *The Decameron*, and *Medea*, as well as *The Driver's Seat* and the X-rated *Caligula* for *Penthouse* magazine publisher Bob Guccione.

Roberto Rossellini (1906-1977), who learned moviemaking at Cinecittà, made his first feature film in 1941, then earned international acclaim with the neorealist classic *Open City* in 1945. The picture was made on the streets of Rome with mostly non-professional actors. Its poor film stock gave it a documentary quality, and Rossellini's next effort, *Paisa*, also a major success, delivered what film critic James Agee called "the illusion of the present tense." Rossellini films were not suitable as Hollywood products, and he continued—contentedly—to work in Europe.

Gioacchino Rossini is best known for his opera *Il Barbiere di Siviglia* and for the music from *Guillaume Tell* (William Tell) used for *The Lone Ranger*. When the composer—born in 1792 in Pesaro on Italy's Adriatic coast—retired at 37 he'd created 39 operas. He retired early because he'd started early: at six he was playing music in a band, at 12 publishing compositions, and at 18 saw his first opera performed. The 600-page score for *The Barber of Seville* (1816) took him 13 days to write.

Rossini moved to Paris in 1824 and died there in 1868 but was reburied in Florence in 1887.

Angelo Rossitto's (1908-1999) specialty was horror movies; he made several with Bela Lugosi. Born Angelo Salvatore Rossitto in Omaha and sometimes billed as Little Angie, he grew to only 2'11" (89 cm.). Discovered for silent movies by John Barrymore, Angelo was active from 1927 to 1987. He appeared in the 1930s films *Freaks* and *Dante's Inferno*, was a stuntman for Shirley Temple, and did over 100 TV shows, including a recurring role on *Barretta* in the 1970s.

Though Rossitto was seen in over 200 motion pictures and TV programs, he often had no lines and was used for visual effect. His work on a given project usually took one day or less. He made his living from the Hollywood newsstand he operated from the 1930s to the 1960s and was a cofounder of Little People of America. Last employed in a movie starring Vincent Price, Angelo did not choose to retire; his increasing blindness and age made him uninsurable.

Nino Rota (1911-1979) composed the scores for over 150 motion pictures between 1933 and 1979. Giovanni Rota

Rinaldi, born in Milan, worked most often with directors Federico Fellini and Luchino Visconti, but won an Oscar for *The Godfather Part II* (1974; he scored the first two *Godfather* movies). His sound could be (of course) Fellini-esque or sweeping, lyrical or contemporary, "Italian" or international. Its diversity is evidenced in *War and Peace* (1956), *Death on the Nile* (1976), *Apocalypse Now* (1979), and his last, *Hurricane* (1979).

Rota also taught at the Liceo Musicale in Bari, Italy, where he held the post of director for nearly 30 years, and he composed ten operas, five ballets, dozens of orchestral, choral, and chamber works, plus much music for theatre productions.

Johnny Roventini (1910-1998) was called "a living trademark" and "an advertising giant." The Brooklyn-born immigrants' son was a 47-inch, 59-lb. real-life bellboy in 1933 when he was cast for commercials to announce, using a perfect B-flat tone, "Call for Philip Morris!" an estimated one million times in decades to come. Wearing a bellboy's short jacket, piped trousers, pillbox hat, and white gloves, "Johnny" performed in countless print, radio, and TV ads. When first approached, Roventini didn't know "Philip Morris" referred to a cigarette. He didn't accept the offer until he received the okay of his mother, with whom he lived much of his life—a "confirmed bachelor," as the saying went.

Johnny eventually earned $50,000 a year, a big salary then, and was lent a small chauffeured convertible to get to his live broadcasts on time. Philip Morris was *I Love Lucy*'s sole sponsor from its 1951 debut until 1954, due to corporate bigotry about Lucille Ball being married onscreen and in real life to a Cuban and a Catholic.

Roventini retired in 1974, after over 40 years as a company mascot and actor.

Salami is sausage cured with salt and spices, fermented and air-dried, from a variety of ground animal meats. Salami became popular long ago because once cut it could be stored at room temperature for 30 to 40 days. Salami is the plural of salame, the word deriving from sale—salt—as in salted meats. The long, thin sausage is usually encased in animal intestine. Variations of salami are sometimes named after their place of origin, e.g., Genovese and Milanese. One of the most famous is peperone, which, thinly sliced, is the most popular meat topping on pizza.

Antonio Salieri's (1750-1825) name reached a wider public via the Oscar-winning *Amadeus* (1984), which garnered F. Murray Abraham a Best Actor Academy Award as the great antagonist and competitor to Wolfgang Amadeus Mozart in Vienna. The film exaggerated Salieri's antagonism and, as did an opera by Rimsky-Korsakov, spread the myth that a jealous Salieri slowly poisoned his genius rival. In fact he frequently came to the younger man's fiscal rescue, organized and conducted a requiem mass for Mozart, and helped Amadeus's son pursue a musical career.

Born in Lombardy, at age 16 Salieri emigrated to Vienna, where he held important posts and composed 39 operas, several sonatas and concertos, and two symphonies. A sought-after teacher, he taught Liszt, Schubert, and Beethoven. In 1824 he did become mentally ill, was institutionalized, and died the following year.

Saltimbocca alla Romana. The name of this dish associated with Rome but possibly originating in Brescia means "leap in the mouth." It's veal scallopine layered with fresh sage leaves and prosciutto crudo, quickly fried in butter with white wine or Marsala.

Scaloppina is a thin pounded slice of meat, most commonly served alla Marsala, with Marsala wine, or al limone, with lemon juice.

Sambuca is a licorice-flavored Roman liqueur, often called anisetta. Traditionally it's served with coffee beans floating in the glass—sambuca con le mosche ("with flies"). Sambuca is made with the flowers of the sambuco bush; they're also used in soup and fritters.

San Marino is the oldest and tiniest continuous republic on earth and Europe's third-smallest country. San Marino lies entirely inside Italy, 12 miles west of Rimini on the Adriatic coast. Legend says it was founded by St. Marinus and his followers in 301 CE. San Marino covers 23.6 square miles and has about 30,000 inhabitants. It was an independent free city by 1351; the pope granted it recognition in 1503, and in 1862 a recently independent Italy ratified a treaty that again recognized the republic's independence.

In 1861 San Marino made Abraham Lincoln an honorary citizen. His acceptance letter noted, "Although your dominion is small, nevertheless your state is one of the most honored throughout history." During World War II it remained neutral. San Marino gave asylum to some 100,000 refugees escaping Nazi and Fascist persecution.

Sandwiches. Italy's are among the best anywhere, primarily because of the breads. A panino is a small bread, and a paninoteca is a sandwich shop where the aromatic product may be stuffed with ham or other meats, seafood, cheeses, condiments, eggs, nuts, vegetables, solo or in endless combinations. The paninoteca, like so much else in modern Italy, began in Milan. The selection of breads—from focaccia to rolls to actually delicious white bread, etc.—may be toasted or not and varies from region to region. In Rome the crustless tramezzino (triangle-cut) sandwich rules, while in Bologna local crusty rolls called rosette are favored. With sandwiches like these, who would choose Jack-in-the-Box?

Sanremo Music Festival, or Festival della Canzone Italiana di Sanremo is an annual competition of new songs that began in 1951. It's a composer's, not a singer's competition, thus for many years each song was sung twice by different artists with different arrangements—traditionally an Italian singer and an international guest singer. The festival, which inspired the Eurovision Song Contest, has launched the careers of several famous Italian singers.

Santa Maria Della Salute church in Venice is sometimes said to look like it's made of white chocolate. Opposite the water from Piazza San Marco and the Doge's Palace, it's a stunning specimen of classical Baroque. Commenced in 1631, it commemorated the city's surviving the worst of the plague of 1630. Architect Baldassare Longhena (1598-1682) designed it as an octagon with a tall dome, high columns, scrolls, volutes, and over 100 exterior statues. But from a distance the impression is rounded and bulging, cloud-like or pastry-like. The ethereal temple was completed five years after Longhena's death.

Lucky Santangelo is novelist Jackie Collins's most popular character, around whom she's written seven novels—and a cookbook with many an Italian recipe. Bold and beautiful, Lucky is the daughter of a former gangster named Gino and the mother of a promising teenage daughter named Max. Says Collins, "Lucky inspires women to be stronger. She is a positive role model…a true female superhero."

Sardinian Music-Paper Bread. On the island of Sardinia, after which sardines were named, paper and bread used to be rolled up for more convenient storage. The large local unleavened sheets of paper-thin bread were called carta da musica, music paper. Sardinians still break the sheets into smaller pieces to eat with meals or as a snack with olive oil or soft goat or sheep's cheese, or to dunk or crumble into soup, or layer them with sauces like pasta. As the bread keeps very well, shepherds still take it along to the pastures.

Father Guido Sarducci, created by actor-writer Don Novello, came to fame on *Saturday Night Live* in the late 1970s. The chain-smoking, mustachioed, tinted-eyeglass-wearing priest was the gossip columnist/rock critic for the Vatican newspaper *L'Osservatore Romano* and later assistant managing editor of *The Vatican Enquirer*. He told of meeting the pope and then experiencing "post-papal depression," and initiated the famous "Find the Pope in the Pizza" contest. The guido father informed viewers, "The take at the shrines in Italy has gone down." His solution: "Shrinemobiles, to take the shrines to the people." Sarducci appeared on other TV shows, did two comedy albums and ads for *High Times* magazine in which he offered to perform blessings for a fee.

Novello's sister-in-law Dr. Antonia Coello Novello was a U.S. Surgeon General.

Alla puttanesca, meaning prostitute style—bold, with tomatoes, chili peppers, garlic, onions, capers, anchovies, and oregano.

Sauces A favorite Italian American dish is Chicken Cacciatore, often served with marinara sauce rather than the alla cacciatora kind (in Italy this dish sometimes excludes tomatoes). In either country it's often served with pasta or a rustic bread on the side. The North American version's sauce frequently includes bell pepper. Braised rabbit used occasionally to substitute for chicken, less so nowadays.

> Italian tomato sauces vary deliciously in style and by region. To name a few:
>
> All'arrabiata means enraged style, spicy, made with chili peppers, tomato, and pancetta, typically served with penne pasta.
>
> Alla cacciatora is hunter style, traditionally tomato sauce with wild mushrooms over sautéed and braised meats, especially game.
>
> Alla diavola means devil style, also heavily spiced, with chili peppers or black pepper. Often served with chicken.
>
> Alla marinara, mariner's style, usually on pasta. The ingredients vary but typically involve crushed tomatoes, olive oil, garlic, oregano, or other herbs.

Scampi has assorted meanings, all to do with crustaceans. It may mean a large shrimp boiled or sautéed. The Italian word is the plural of scampo, a prawn. "Scampi" is most often found on North American restaurant menus, usually following "shrimp." It was introduced to Britain in 1946 when an Italian restaurant substituted it for lobster. In the UK it's often battered, deep-fried shelled tail meat, served with tartar sauce.

In Italy, preparations vary regionally, but shrimp scampi is typically prepared in garlic butter and dry white wine, served with bread to sop up the juice or over pasta or rice, occasionally alone. The garlic and butter sauce may be adapted to lobster, crab, etc.

Angelina Scarangella was, believe it or not, Barbara Joan Streisand's alias before she became Barbra Streisand. The budding singer-actress from Brooklyn felt herself an outsider and initially shied away from her own name. She identified with Chinese and Italian culture—the former partly because she worked in a Chinese restaurant and loved the food, the latter because of its culture, language, food, and Italian chic. When Sophia Loren met Streisand and told her she wished she could sing like her, Barbra replied, "If I looked like you, I wouldn't even bother to open my mouth."

Elsa Schiaparelli's (1890-1973) astronomer uncle Giovanni discovered the "canali" of Mars. Born in Rome to upper-crust parents, Elsa was sent to a convent where she later escaped by going on a hunger strike. At 22 she moved to London as a nanny, then to New York, then settled in Paris, where she befriended and later collaborated with artists in the Dada and Surrealist movements. Between the two world wars, the House of Schiaparelli, opened in the 1930s, was a leading fashion influence. The only major female rival to "Schiap" (pronounced Skap) was Gabrielle "Coco" Chanel.

In her heyday, Schiaparelli was innovative and bold. She created wraparound dresses and the first evening dress with a jacket, also the first clothes with visible zippers. Her perfumes made a show of their unusual bottles and packaging. When Elsa designed the movie costumes for *Every Day's a Holiday* (1937), Mae West's mannequin provided the inspiration for the torso bottle containing Schiaparelli's "Shocking" perfume. The designer's signature color was "shocking pink."

After WWII, Schiap failed to move with the times. Dior launched The New Look, but Elsa tied herself to nostalgia and in 1954 her business shut its doors.

Martin Scorsese, born in 1942, was part of the Hollywood New Wave that included Italian American filmmakers like Coppola and De Palma. A director, writer, producer, and film preservationist, in 1990 Scorsese established The Film Foundation to that end. Among the varied pictures he's directed are *Mean Streets*, *Taxi Driver*, *Raging Bull*, *Casino*, *Kundun*, *Alice Doesn't Live Here Anymore*; *New York, New York*; *Gangs of New York*, *The Wolf of Wall Street*, and *The Irishman*.

A number of his films have explored the Italian American experience, and several of them starred friend Robert De Niro and more recently, Leonardo Di Caprio. Two of Scorsese's five wives were actress Isabella Rossellini and producer Barbara De Fina. Of his eight Oscar nominations, he won Best Director for *The Departed*.

Semolina is from the Italian word semola, meaning bran (also freckle), deriving from the Latin *simila*, flour. It's the coarse, purified wheat middlings of durum wheat used to make pasta, breakfast cereals, and puddings. Semolina can also refer to rice and corn. Semolina from durum wheat is yellow; when semolina is made from softer kinds of wheat, it's white and is actually flour. In the U.S. coarser meal from softer wheat is called farina—which is flour in Italian.

Boiled semolina resembles Cream of Wheat. In Italy semolina puddings are a tasty and wholesome dessert, with several variations: for instance, instance served with red currant sauce or blueberry sauce, or whipped semolina laced with bits of fruit or semolina cooked in cream, which has a pudding-like texture and may be drizzled with honey or myrtle sauce or…the only limit is one's imagination.

Sfumato. Every art student knows the word chiaroscuro, Italian for light/dark. It refers to the chromatic contrast between light and dark and is strongly associated with Renaissance painters. Sfumato means shaded or evaporated like smoke and is a subtle, even barely perceptible way of transitioning between colors and tones. It can also help create a mood and is most often used to describe aspects of Leonardo da Vinci's paintings, for instance in the curves of the Mona Lisa's hair and clothing, echoed in the shapes of the valleys and rivers behind her.

Shakespeare. One of the prime arguments against the humble man from Stratford having penned the Shakespeare plays is that their author almost had to be a highly educated, wealthy, and well-traveled aristocrat, with special knowledge of the Italian scene. Various Shakespearian plays are set in Mantua, Padua, Verona, etc., and the playwright knew northern Italy's geography and customs quite well. No evidence connects the man from Stratford with writing, only with acting, while some of the contenders for "the real Shakespeare"—who may have been a pair or group of writers using the Stratford man as a front due to royal censorship—had indeed sojourned or resided, on behalf of Elizabeth I's government, in Italy.

Sic. How useful is that? This wee Latin word means *so* or *thus*. Used in brackets, it indicates that the preceding word is spelled exactly that way, even if it looks odd or wrong (of course, one should be certain of the preceding word's spelling!). Using (sic) avoids a wordy explanation.

Example: inglorious is spelled thus, and bastards like that. But Quentin Tarantino's 2009 movie title deliberately misspelled them *Inglourious Basterds* (sic).

Words and terms like sic whose English translations are longer tend to endure, including ones we may not realize are Latin because they're now initials, for instance i.e. and e.g. Other long-used Latin terms are falling by the wayside, like *per diem* (per day), *per annum* (per year), and *per capita* (per person), though less so in legalese, off and on the telly—e.g., *habeas corpus* and *in flagrante delicto*.

Singers—more female Italian Americans.

- Ani DiFranco is a singer, songwriter, multi-instrumentalist musician, poet, and social activist with her own record label. Though much of her music is alternative and folk rock, she crosses musical genres and has released over 20 albums since her debut in 1990. She was born in 1970.

- Eydie Gorme (1928-2013) was born Edith Gormezano to Sephardic Jewish parents—a Sicilian father and Turkish mother. Gorme performed solo and with husband Steve Lawrence. Her biggest hit was "Blame It on the Bossa Nova," and she won a Grammy for "If He Walked Into My Life." She enjoyed great success singing in Spanish for the Latin American market.

- Cyndi Lauper (born in 1953 of a Sicilian mother) became the first woman, in 2013, to win solo (or sola) the Tony Award for Best Original Score, for the Broadway musical *Kinky Boots*. Cyndi's 1983 debut album *She's So Unusual* was the first by a female singer to chart four Top-Five hits, including her iconic "Girls Just Wanna Have Fun."

- Nancy Sinatra had a string of groovy '60s hits, from "Sugartown," "Bang Bang," and "These Boots Are

Made for Walkin'" to one of the most beautiful James Bond theme songs, "You Only Live Twice." Born in 1940, she appeared in eight 1960s movies.

But also Liza Minnelli, Patti LuPone, Carol Lawrence (Carol Maria Laraia), Toni Basil, Laura Nyro (Laura Nigra), Gwen Stefani, Dodie Stevens (Geraldine Ann Pasquale), Suzi Quatro, and Morgana King, born Maria Grazia Morgana Messina (mamma mia!).

Singers—more male Italian Americans.

- Perry Como (originally Pierino; 1912-2001), an easy-going ex-barber, failed in Hollywood but became a major recording and television star. Nicknamed Mr. C., his many hits included "Till the End of Time," "Papa Loves Mambo," and "For the Good Times."
- Julius La Rosa's big break was being fired live on Arthur Godfrey's top-rated TV show in 1953—because he'd made a record without Godfrey's permission! Among his hits: "Anywhere I Wander," "Three Coins in the Fountain," and "Eh, Cumpari," which reached #1. La Rosa was born in 1930.
- Frankie Laine (born Francesco Paolo LoVecchio; 1913-2007) was a singer-songwriter-actor. Aka Mr. Rhythm, his seven-decades-plus recording career was dominated by western hits like "Mule Train," "Rawhide," and the theme song from "High Noon."

- Bobby Rydell's major hits included "Wild One," "Volare," and "Sway." He's best remembered from the movie musical *Bye Bye Birdie* (1963), which made a star of Ann-Margret. Like several boy singers, he was born in Philadelphia (in 1942) — as Robert Ridarelli.

But also don't forget Canadian Gino Vanelli and Americans Jon Bon Jovi and Richie Sambora, Frank Zappa, Jim Croce, Al Martino, and half Italians — via their unnamed mothers — Don McLean, Chris Isaak, John Oates of Hall and Oates, and, among others, Bruce Springsteen.

Singing, it's been said, is embedded in the Italian soul. Italy is the home of opera and the world's most famous opera house and has produced many of its greatest opera singers. Also, far more Italian songs than are generally known have been re-lyricized into hit songs in English. Polls say that more Italians believe they are good singers than people in English-speaking countries do. Oscar-winner Anna Magnani felt she received a second nomination (for *Wild Is the Wind*, 1957) because "People in Hollywood liked very much how I sang in one scene...a beautiful and traditional Italian song. I sing it well, but most people who sing it do also."

In some of her Italian movies, Sophia Loren sang. "One American director said to me, 'I didn't know you could sing.' Eh, you have to be professionally trained? No. I said, 'Of course I can sing. I am Italian.'"

Soccer's modern version began in Britain in the 1850s. In Renaissance Florence a form of football was played by the aristocracy as a contest in connection with Shrove Tuesday. Reportedly, the "ball" was sometimes an enemy's severed head. The earliest proto-soccer was played in eastern Mexico by the Olmecs over 3,500 years ago. The Olmecs devised the first bouncing balls, via rubber. Ball games were vital sporting and ritual events among the Mayas and Aztecs, and when Europeans arrived in Mexico in the 1520s they were shocked and frightened by the bouncing balls, which many believed were animated by "the devil."

British influence on soccer—calcio, in Italian—is still apparent in Italy, where the game was first played in the northern cities of Genoa, Milan, and Turin. Juventus of Turin wear black-and-white striped shirts originally modeled on those of the English club Notts County. Genoa and Milan have teams with anglicized names, and AC Milan was formed in 1899 as the Milan Cricket and Football Club by Englishman Alfred Edwards. The club was for English sportsmen and rich Milanese residents.

The globe's soccer-champ nations are Germany, Brazil, and Italy. Italy won the World Cup in 1934, 1938, 1982, and 2006, and has nearly always placed in the finals. Actor Vittorio Gassman believed, "We like soccer best of all games because it is just your body and a ball—direct contact. No bat or club, no gloves or bumping into each other on purpose, no advantage from one's height. It is about true skill and what the individual spirit can achieve in an unforeseen moment."

According to soccer icon Roberto Biaggio, "We don't only think about it when a match is scheduled or during a season. For many Italians it is year-round—like a soccer culture." Italian soccer matches are often entertainment spectacles, with special songs, waving of elaborate flags, orchestrated slogans, and choreographed waves and movements. Says soccer star Paolo Rossi, "Time, thought, and money can go into being a fan." Soccer, money, and charity may go together too. The sale of clods of turf from the Olympic Stadium in Rome where the 1990 World Cup final was held netted $5.8 million, and in 1996 Italian male strippers formed a national soccer team to play for charity—coached by former pro player Enzo Romano.

The downside of soccer culture or mania? During the 1988 European championships nearly the whole staff of San Gennaro Hospital in Naples abandoned patients to watch a match between Italy and Sweden in Naples. Thirty-nine hospital employees were arrested and criminal charges were filed against 200 more.

The South of Italy has long been more agriculturally oriented and poorer than the North. But natives often say this is the real Italy, that the North and its industrial centers are but extensions of Europe, i.e., France, Switzerland, Austria.

"They of the North know how to make money," opined actor Adolfo Celi, best known as the eye-patched villain in the James Bond classic *Thunderball*. "But we make better food, we make better music, we enjoy life more. We have the heart. Maybe the colder weather up there makes them colder, I don't know."

Southern emigrants. Most Italian emigrants to the U.S. and elsewhere come from Italy's less affluent South. Ergo, southern Italian cuisine—especially Neapolitan—is better known abroad (as with China, whose mostly southern emigrants have spread Cantonese cuisine worldwide). Ergo too, the stereotype of the dark-haired and -eyed, swarthy Italian, more typical, for instance, of Sicily, which ignores—especially in Hollywood pictures—millions of pale, light-haired, sometimes blue-eyed northerners.

Northern movie producer Carlo Ponti (*Doctor Zhivago*), married to southern movie star Sophia Loren, summed it up: "From the North, progress. From the South, essence."

Spaghetti. Its name is the diminutive of spago, or string. Spaghetti's strings are between macaroni and vermicelli in thickness. Compared to many Italian dishes, spaghetti is a relative newcomer, at least in its "modern" version with tomato sauce.

Sophia Loren once said of herself, tongue in cheek, "Everything you see I owe to spaghetti."

Spaghettini is a thinner spaghetti. A spaghetti strap is a thin rounded shoulder strap on women's clothing, and spaghettification is the physics theory that an object which fell into a black hole would be pulled and ripped apart via gravitational forces.

Spaghetti and meatballs. First, until recently it was seldom served as a complete meal in Italy—with or without meatballs or meat sauce, etc. Second, spaghetti and meatballs, certainly a meal in itself, was invented in the U.S. by immigrants from southern Italy. It is thus the Italian American dish *par excellence*.

Spaghetti westerns were a 1960s Italian phenomenon, occasionally filmed in Spain and often starring Americans, that caught on internationally. The genre's major exponent was Sergio Leone. Henry Fonda, who actually played a villain in *Once Upon a Time in the West* (1968), offered, "Sergio's bolder, more violent take on the Old West is probably truer to life than what we're used to."

Perhaps the best known spaghetti westerns were Leone's Dollars trilogy: *A Fistful of Dollars*, *For a Few Dollars More* and *The Good, the Bad and the Ugly*. In them, Sergio took a chance on a U.S. TV actor who hadn't made a movie in six years—Hollywood saw no potential in him—named Clint Eastwood. Reportedly, Sophia Loren apprised Eastwood in California that his Italian vehicles were cleaning up in Europe, which fact he used as leverage to re-launch his screen career in Hollywood.

Eastwood's 1992 western *Unforgiven* that won him a Best Director Oscar was co-dedicated "To Sergio."

Spumante. Almost one billion bottles of this sweet, sparkling, low-alcohol dessert wine are produced annually, mostly around the city of Asti, Piedmont. Italy's answer to champagne, it's used to celebrate weddings, holidays, the New Year, and much else.

Another Piedmont wine is dolcetto, a fruity, less sweet wine—its name means a little sweet. Dolcetto is intended for early consumption, as it doesn't improve with aging.

Spumoni derives from spuma, or foam. Egg yolks, cooked with hot sugar syrup to create a thick custard, make spumoni creamier than regular gelato. Despite the yolks, spumoni is light and airy thanks to the egg foam and whipped cream. Spumoni is molded, in layers of different colors, often containing candied fruits and nuts. The most typical flavors are cherry, pistachio, and chocolate or vanilla, so the usual color scheme is pink, green, brown.

August 21 is National Spumoni Day in the USA, as is November 13 in Canada.

Stadio Giuseppe Meazza in Milan, still often called by its old name of San Siro, was renamed after a soccer star crucial to Italy's winning the 1938 World Cup by scoring on a penalty kick seconds before his ripped shorts fell to his ankles in a semifinals match against Brazil. Many believed Meazza intentionally let his shorts fall to distract the goalkeeper. In any case, Italy won 2-1 to advance to the final.

The stadium is home to AC Milan and Internazionale Milan, which were Milan FC until 1908 when several members broke away to protest British influence over the club, renaming themselves Internazionale. At its maximum the stadium seated 88,500, now 80,500 in keeping with the trend toward fewer seats for better crowd control. Its overhaul for the 1990 World Cup included an overhanging roof then praised as an architectural innovation. Stadio Giuseppe Meazza is known for its intimacy and atmosphere; however, the roof doesn't allow enough sun or rain to reach the field often enough to let grass take root. That, combined with Milan's misty, foggy weather, often produces muddy playing conditions.

Sylvester Stallone's first movie was the X-rated *Party at Kitty and Stud's* before he endured bit parts supporting Woody Allen, Jack Lemmon and Anne Bancroft (*née* Anna Maria Italiano), and Robert Mitchum. Then Sly wrote a screenplay, *Rocky*, a hot property he would only sell if the studio let him play the title role, which they did in 1976.

(Brother Frank Stallone has had a lower-key acting-and-music career.)

Stereotypes endure because they usually contain a kernel of truth. However, repeated, unkind exaggeration is limiting, even harmful. It gives the majority a false impression that they know more about a given people than they do. But there are stereotypes and stereotypes. Actor-comedian Mario Cantone explains, "Da Vinci, the greatest genius of all time, was Italian. We invented the Renaissance and the best food on earth. And opera—well, nobody's perfect. So we talk with our hands; that's a better stereotype than strong and silent, which usually means dumb and aloof."

Singer Jerry Vale (*né* Genaro Louis Vitaliano) recalled "the days when you had to hide your Italian name....How good is a melting pot if it melts your identity and tries to shame you? I applaud the young people who're proud of who they are."

Cantone concludes, "I'm Italian and I'm gay, so I'm allowed to be as loud as I want! I'm not a genius, but da Vinci was Italian and gay too, and I never read that he was loud. Anyhow, better a visible stereotype than soul-crushing invisibility."

Stra maze. The maze of the Villa Pisani about 18 miles (27 km.) southwest of Venice is far bigger. It's a huge tourist attraction, in both senses of the word: a third the size of a U.S. football field, with four miles of hedgerow-protected paths in which nearly everybody gets lost. The 168-room villa was commissioned in 1735 by a Venetian doge and boasts ceilings painted by Tiepolo. Umpteen celebrities have gotten lost in the labyrinth, including actors, kings, and emperors (Napoleon, for one). When Mussolini and Hitler held a summit at Villa Pisani in 1934 they avoided navigating the maze, for fear of looking foolish.

During the tourist season a caretaker watches from the top of a tower in the center of the maze, ready to shout directions to the lost and so that new visitors may be admitted.

Stracchino is among the most popular northern Italian cheeses. Its name comes from stracca, meaning tiredness. Rural legend held that the milk of tired cows, trudging to and from Alpine pastures during the seasonal move, contains more fats and acids, giving this cheese its tang. Stracchino is usually enjoyed as a dessert cheese.

Stracciatella is the diminutive of straccia—shred. Stracciatella alla Romana is an egg-drop soup that may include Parmesan cheese, nutmeg, lemon zest, sometimes semolina, and salt and pepper. It can be served in bowls containing Melba-type toast with extra grated Parmesan on top. It was described in Martino da Como's fifteenth-century book *The Art of Cooking*.

Stracciatella is also a soft, stretched-curd cheese that employs a shredding technique originated in Apulia in southeastern Italy. There is also a stracciatella variety of gelato, seeded with chocolate flakes, invented in Bergamo, northern Italy, in 1962.

Strega, a liqueur whose name means "witch," was mentioned several times in Mario Puzo's *The Godfather*. Relatively new, it's been produced in Benevento, Campania, since 1860. Less bright yellow than Galliano, its color is reportedly owed to saffron, one of Strega's 70 or so herbal ingredients, including mint and fennel. Strega is considered a *digestif* for after meals. It's also used to flavor Torta Caprese cake and was once believed by many to be a love potion.

Italy's most prestigious literary prize is the Premio Strega, founded in 1947 by Strega's owner. Seems strange? The Nobel Prizes, including the Peace Prize, are by way of a dynamite manufacturer.

Surnames. Italy's ten most common surnames apply to only about one percent of the population. Italian last names aren't just seemingly innumerable, they're sometimes bizarre, like Occhiofino (Keen-eye), Bellagamba (Beautiful-leg, the name of a famous cardinal), Malatesta (Bad-head), and Mezzasalma (Half-corpse). Often they're food-related—Bevilacqua (Drink-the-water), Mangiafico (Eat-fig), Mangiacavallo (Eat-horse), Gattamelata (Honey-cat), Tagliabue (Ox-cutter), and Pancioni (Big-bellies).

Italo Svevo was born in Trieste, where he became a banker. His birth name was Ettore Schmitz (1861-1928) and his writing began as a hobby. His well-crafted novels include his first, *A Life* (1892), and *As a Man Grows Older* (1898) and *The Confessions of Zeno* (1923). They were ahead of their time in terms of dwelling on the middle class and focusing on introspection and self-analysis. Thus, the Jewish Svevo was virtually ignored until he was "discovered" by Irishman James Joyce, who was his English teacher at the Berlitz school in Trieste.

Swept Away is proof that Italians often do movies better. The 1974 film, fully titled *Swept Away by an Unusual Destiny in the Blue Sea of August* and written and directed by Lina Wertmuller, became an international hit and cult classic. It starred Mariangela Melato and Giancarlo Giannini.

The 2002 English-language remake starred Madonna and Giannini's son Adriano and was directed by Ms. Ciccone's then-husband, Englishman Guy Ritchie. Reviews were dismal or worse, and the $10 million production earned under $600,000 in the U.S. and killed off Madonna's anemic movie career.

Melato's character was named Raffaella Pavone Lanzetti. Madonna's was Amber Leighton—how Anglo can you get?

Tagliatelle are long, flat pasta ribbons reputedly inspired by the long, blonde, below-her-knees hairstyle of Lucrezia Borgia, who met a delighted chef at the court of the d'Este family upon her arrival to wed Alfonso I. The d'Estes ruled Ferrara for about three centuries, until the pope forced them to move to Modena in 1598; as for the marriage, Lu had an affair with her bisexual brother-in-law.

Native, nonetheless, to Bologna, tagliatelle are made with egg, and if green, with spinach, and may be served with a ragu-type sauce or butter and cheese. The Accademia Italiana della Cucina (Italian Academy of Cooking) set tagliatelle's dimensions at 8 mm (5/16") wide and .6 mm (1/32") thick. A golden replica of one is housed in Bologna's city hall. The noodle name comes from tagliare, to cut, and variations include tagliardi, taglione, tagliolini, and tagliarini.

Luisa Tetrazzini was a top opera star from the 1890s into the 1920s. From 1907, after a sensational British debut playing Violetta in *La Traviata*, Tetrazzini (1871-1940) was an international star. Born in Florence, the coloratura soprano was short and became progressively heavier, sometimes drawing criticism for her inappropriate roles—e.g., the consumptive Mimi in *La Boheme.*

Her golden years were spoiled by poor health and poverty; her third husband squandered her money. More than once she asseverated, "I am old, I am fat, but I am still Tetrazzini."

> Turkey Tetrazzini was probably created in San Francisco, where Luisa Tetrazzini lived for a time, by the chef of the Palace Hotel in 1904 or between 1908 and 1910 (sources vary). The recipe usually includes turkey chunks, noodles, mushrooms, and Parmesan cheese. One reason it became popular in the U.S. is it's a great way to use up Thanksgiving leftovers.
>
> Tetrazzini dishes without turkey differ widely but often include an Alfredo sauce.

Tiramisu. The name of this now internationally beloved dessert is literally "pick me up." It may also be a pick-me-up after the caffeine jolt from its espresso coffee and chocolate! Tiramisu's birthplace—possibly Treviso—is debatable. It comes in several versions, sometimes a heavier one that mixes raw egg yolks with mascarpone cheese. Some recipes employ zabaglione for the custard or cream element, others whipped cream and mascarpone. Some use cocoa or grated bitter chocolate, others exclude the coffee. The alcohol may be brandy, rum, or any Italian flavored liqueur. The sponge fingers are soaked in the coffee, rum, or brandy and layered with the chosen cream and the cocoa or chocolate.

Tiziano (1488-1576) actually Tiziano Vecellio, was, like Michelangelo Buonnaroti, best known by his first name. It is also now the name of a hair color—bright golden auburn (reddish brown)—due to its frequency in his paintings. In his lifetime, Tiziano was as well known as Michelangelo; some experts believe him the better painter. Art historian Luciano Mangiafico noted his "splendid results using his brushes to create light and shadow and particular moods. He was meticulous and applied many layers of glaze to his paintings, often 30 to 40, until he was satisfied with their richness of color and shimmering tonality."

Politically astute, Tiziano did portraits of several kings and popes, eventually acquiring wealth and his own Venetian palace. Michelangelo suffered lifelong jealousy, opining that his junior didn't even know how to draw! Tiziano's influence is evident in the work of Rembrandt, El Greco, Rubens, Van Dyck, and others.

Ugo Tognazzi (1922-1990), born in Cremona, worked in a salami factory before acting in theatre, TV, and film, including *Barbarella* and *Fellini Satyricon*. He became internationally famous as Renato Baldi, partner of Albin Mougeotte, aka drag queen Zaza Napoli, in *La Cage Aux Folles* (1978). The Franco-Italian movie directed by Edouard Molinaro spawned sequels in 1980 and '85, and in 1983 became a hit Broadway musical which renamed Renato Georges.

In 1996 Hollywood retitled the project *The Birdcage*, relocated to Miami from St. Tropez, with Robin Williams as the renamed Armand. Though this version too dealt in stereotypes, the core story still had heart and again inspired the performances.

Topo Gigio was arguably the most popular guest on *The Ed Sullivan Show*, appearing some 50 times on the star-studded TV variety series. Ten inches tall with doe-like eyes cut from foam rubber, Topo (Italian for mouse) Gigio (a nickname for Luigi, or Louis) could talk, walk, roll his eyes, wiggle his ears and toes and gesture—all at the same time.

He was created by Maria Perego Caldura of Milan, who performed all his movements except for his hands and arms, which two other also unseen puppeteers controlled while a fourth individual supplied the cuddly rodent's voice.

Topo Gigio, who starred in his own children's TV series and movie and was marketed as a doll, a puppet, on t-shirts, towels, etc., etc., remains molto popular in his home country.

Tortellini are small rings of pasta filled with ground pork, veal, prosciutto, mortadella, Parmigiano, and nutmeg. Or sometimes just cheese. They may be served in broth or a white sauce and hail from the Emilia region, particularly Bologna and Modena. One myth says tortellini are turtle-shaped in homage to Modena's numerous seventeenth-century buildings that have a turtle motif. In English, tortellini are sometimes called "belly buttons" due to their supposed navel shape. Tortelloni are a larger variation, with vegetable stuffing.

Tortoni, a frozen dessert created in Paris by a Neapolitan, comprises whipped cream, sweetened and flavored, to which is added something of almond, whether chopped almonds or crumbled amaretto cookies, and possibly chopped maraschino cherries, etc. The cream may be flavored with rum, sherry, or a liqueur like Amaretto. The concoction is frozen till firm, then allowed to soften slightly.

Tortoni's. In 1798 Neapolitan Giuseppe Tortoni, 23, arrived in Paris and bought an apparently failing café from a fellow Italian named Velloni. Tortoni renamed it after himself, and for 95 years—located at 22, Boulevard des Italiens—was the "in" place in Paris for cold Italian desserts. Manet did a painting titled "Chez Tortoni" that was one of 13 artworks stolen from Boston's Isabelle Stewart Gardner Museum in 1990 by two men posing as policemen.

When Tortoni arrived in Paris he brought "an ancient and ailing mother, an ugly and bothersome wife, three ill-mannered children, and a sway-backed horse, the only member of my family who has any sympathies for my ambitions." In 1864, at 89, Tortoni wrote, "My children, although now adults, remain ill-mannered and I fear for the fate of my little establishment once I am gone and it falls into their hands." It didn't close until 1893.

Arturo Toscanini (1867-1957) was a, or the, musical conductor from 1886 to 1954, all the more remarkable in view of the myriad enemies the talented, temperamental egotist accrued. Because he always conducted from his fantastic memory, ill-wishers declared he couldn't read music very well. His repertoire numbered 117 operas and 480 orchestral pieces by 228 composers.

In 1931 Toscanini declined to play the official Fascist hymn and was beaten up by Mussolini's thugs, prompting his emigration to the U.S., where he became first associate conductor, then conductor of the New York Philharmonic. In 1937 he was hired by NBC to form a new orchestra to perform radio concerts. The maestro died in Manhattan at 90 and is buried in Milan.

The little-seen 1988 flop movie *Young Toscanini* starring cowboyish American C. Thomas Howell and Elizabeth Taylor as an astonished opera diva can only be described as an embarrassment.

Travel. Italy received almost 48 million tourists in 2013. Italy is Americans' second-favorite travel destination outside North America. Scottish novelist Muriel Spark, who moved to Rome and was best known for *The Prime of Miss Jean Brodie*, observed, "Americans who visit Italy tend to be those of Italian or partial Italian heritage who come vaguely seeking part of their identity or else they're culture vultures who know exactly what they're seeking."

As English writer Fanny Burney put it, "Traveling is the ruin of all happiness! There's no looking at a building after seeing Italy."

Katharine Hepburn, star of *Summertime* (1955), filmed in Venice, asserted, "Go now! Don't wait. There's lots to see, but it only gets more crowded and more expensive all the time!"

La Traviata ranks among a handful of the greatest and most popular operas. By Giuseppe Verdi from a story by Alexandre Dumas, it bowed in Venice in 1853 and tells (sings) of the love of Violetta and Alfredo. She is a courtesan—traviare means to lead astray. The fly in the ointment is his father, who persuades her to leave his son, regardless of their mutual devotion. After the inevitable misunderstanding, true love triumphs, except that she has tuberculosis and dies. Despite its clichés, *La Traviata's* music and the coveted role for a great singer/actress—e.g., Maria Callas—keep audiences coming back for more. Brava, brava.

By comparison, the clichés in Puccini's *Madame Butterfly* offend national, racial, and religious sensibilities.

John Travolta (born 1954) broke through as a hunky but dense high school student named Vinnie Barbarino in the TV sitcom *Welcome Back, Kotter*. On the big screen, Travolta hit stardom as hunky but dense Tony Manero in *Saturday Night Fever* (1977).

Tuscan dialect, particularly as spoken in Florence, became the basis of standard Italian for several reasons. Tuscany was economically powerful and more advanced than most Italian city-states due to its political and cultural influence—its artists were the crème de la crème—and legacy of Humanism and the Renaissance, not to mention the Medici Bank, Europe's largest.

Italian dialects had gradually replaced Latin as the lingua franca and in many cases the official language of a given city state. In a preface to the 1840 edition of *The Betrothed*, generally considered Italian literature's first modern novel, Alessandro Manzoni wrote that he was "rinsing" his Milanese dialect "in the waters of the Arno," Florence's river.

Tutti Frutti means all fruits and refers to a number of things, for non-Italians have taken up the rhyming, child-like words too—"tutti frutti" was an American chewing gum flavor in 1888. Tutti frutti may be a confection or cookies, often containing cherries, raisins, and pineapple. Or an ice cream flavor. *The Italian Cookbook* (1919) by Marie Gentile offered a recipe for Tutti Frutti Ice that required strawberries, cherries, apricots, peaches, plums, pears, cantaloupe, lemon juice, and powdered sugar. There have been tutti frutti candy bars and soft drinks in various countries, but most usually and probably most deliciously, the words refer to Italian cookies and Italian ice cream.

"Tutti Frutti" was also a mid 1950s song recorded by Elvis Presley, who also did a re-worded English-language version of "O Sole Mio" titled "It's Now or Never."

TV stars—a piccolo sample.

- Alan Alda, son of movie actor Robert (Roberto) Alda, was born in 1936 as Alphonso Joseph D'Abruzzo and is best known as the star of the longrunning series *M*A*S*H*.

- Scott Baio (born in 1960 to immigrant parents) came to fame as Chachi, nephew of Arthur "the Fonz" Fonzarelli on *Happy Days*, costarring in its spin-off, *Joanie Loves Chachi*, and then starring as *Charles in Charge*.

- Tony Danza, like Danny DeVito, was one of the stars made by the hit sitcom *Taxi*, after which he (born in 1951) starred in the sitcom *Who's the Boss?* In 2008 with his son he published *Don't Fill Up on the Antipasto: Tony Danza's Father-Son Cookbook*.

- James Gandolfini (1961-2013) rocketed to fame via *The Sopranos*. The self-described "overstuffed pussycat" noted, "Put me in a supermarket and I can get intimidated by a pushy clerk or cashier. Put me in front of a camera and give me Tony Soprano's dialogue, and I'm off to the races!"

- Susan Lucci (born in 1946) was long the top-paid actor on daytime television, incarnating Erica Kane on the soap opera *All My Children* from 1970 to 2011.
- Marlo Thomas, daughter of Danny Thomas, is Italian on her mother's side. Star of the 1960s single-woman sitcom *That Girl*, she (born in 1937) became a feminist activist and is married to Phil Donahue.

Paolo Uccello the painter loved birds. In those days surnames were optional, and Paolo (1396-1475) chose Uccello, which means bird. As he couldn't afford real birds, he painted them, often. He also loved to experiment with perspective, often drawing items from myriad angles. Today Uccello's work seems less old-fashioned than some of his contemporaries.' He once had to paint over part of a fresco commissioned in Florence after showing the male horse in too much detail. With his specialized interests, Uccello didn't become a wealthy painter, but lived and died in poverty.

A Florentine income tax return revealed he paid no taxes and had no assets. He appended a note to the return: "I am old, infirm, and unemployed—and my wife is ill."

Umberto D. (1952), directed and cowritten by Vittorio De Sica, is a highly touching look at postwar want, old age, quiet pride, loneliness, and love of one's pet. De Sica cast a non-actor professor, Carlo Battisti (his first and last film), as the retired civil servant barely surviving on his pension in a rented room with his dog Flag or Flike (depending on the dubbing). The landlady is shallow and heartless. Umberto Domenico Ferrari tries to get money to pay his rent, even attempting begging, but he can't do it. His dignified struggle to avoid falling from poverty into shame and his platonic relationship with the foolish young housemaid are riveting slices of life. The climax, in which Don Umberto tries to end it all—with Flag in tow—is never to be forgotten. De Sica deemed this neorealist masterpiece (released in the U.S. in 1955) the favorite of his films.

The University of Padua, founded as a law school in 1222, was later also a renowned medical school. Two of its medical alumni boasted stimulating connections with coffee. Venetian Prospero Alpini was a physician who preferred botany. In 1580 he journeyed to Egypt to study its plant life. Back in Padua, he became a professor of botany, publishing his most famous work, *The Plants of Egypt*, in 1592. In it he wrote about coffee, whose medicinal qualities he praised and over-praised.

A decade before, in a formal report, the Venetian ambassador to the Ottoman sultan described the public establishments in Constantinople where men met to socialize and discuss business over the hot black beverage. Public coffeehouses started appearing in Venice and then in other Italian cities. By 1763 Venice counted over 200 of them, and the national tradition continues.

The leading physician of his day, William Harvey studied at the University of Padua and is best known for his 1628 treatise completely explaining, for the first time, the circulation of the blood. At Padua, he'd discovered coffee drinking, which he felt gave him the energy and concentration to tirelessly pursue his studies. Associates remarked his obsession with the beverage, which Harvey declared effective against sloth and drunkenness. He exhorted fellow physicians to forsake beer and wine for coffee, to be better doctors.

Nathaniel Hawthorne's famous short story "Rappaccini's Daughter" (1844) features a University of Padua student and professor.

Valentine's Day. Although they may have been the same person, the Catholic Church lists two St. Valentines with the same feast day of February 14. Little explains why they or he became the patron saint of lovers, a belief dating back to 496 CE. The custom of sending a Valentine to a loved one derives from the fourteenth century as does the notion that birds pair up on February 14th, but the celebration may have begun as the ancient Roman festival of Lupercalia, whose fertility rites fell in mid-February.

Valentino became possibly the most successful and status-y fashion designer outside France via his elegant, expensive clothes and top-end regular clients like Jacqueline Kennedy Onassis, Elizabeth Taylor, the shah of Iran's wife, etc. Born in Voghera in 1932, Valentino Garavani apprenticed with Guy Laroche in Paris, opened a clothing boutique on Rome's Via Condotti in the '50s, and then presided over a dazzling fashion show in Florence in 1962 that set him atop the modiste heap, where he remained for decades to come. He, his designs, and his customers exuded glamour and money. Valentino and his handsome life and business partner Giancarlo Giammetti were careful to expand their empire tastefully and avoid blatant commercialism.

Also, Valentino, Armani, Versace, and most European fashion designers didn't hide being gay, unlike most of their American contemporaries—who, if they wished to be thought heterosexual, why choose this profession?

Rudolph Valentino (1895-1926), the movies' first male sex symbol, enjoyed five years of global superstardom before his early death. His most famous role was *The Sheik* (1921), which even had a sequel—back before sequel-itis. Born in Italy's Puglia region, Rodolfo emigrated to the U.S. in 1913, moving from gardener, waiter, dancer, and reportedly a Manhattan gigolo to Hollywood in 1917, where he broke through four years later. Most female moviegoers loved him, while American males often held him in contempt—too romance-minded, emotional, and foreign.

Ironically, the iconic Latin lover was gay or bisexual. He met both his wives through Alla Nazimova, a lesbian Russian actress-producer who happened to be Nancy Reagan's godmother. His first marriage went unconsummated. When his second wife, a faux Russian from Utah, took over his career and had him wear a "slave bracelet," the male-dominated media, which had never liked him, grew agitated. The "wop" star who did ads for Valvoline Face Cream was labeled "a pink powder puff," etc. Had he lived into the talkie era, it's doubtful whether the fading, heavily accented star's above-the-title career would have survived.

Though he was criticized for the "effeminate" practice, Valentino helped popularize the male wearing of wrist watches.

Frankie Valli was born Francesco Stephen Castelluccio in Newark in 1934. Before turning to singing full-time, he supported himself as a barber. Possessed of a powerful falsetto—a sound the Four Seasons popularized long before the Bee Gees—as the lead singer inevitably drew more of the limelight, the quartet became Frankie Valli and the Four Seasons.

Eventually Valli also took up acting, appearing for instance on several episodes of the HBO TV series *The Sopranos* as mobster Rusty Millio, once referred to as the Mayor of

Munchkinland because of Valli's 5'5" height. Frankie has been honored for his work on behalf of such heritage-related charities as the National Italian American Foundation.

Frankie Valli and the Four Seasons. The original trio of Valli, Nick Massi, and Tommy DeVito wasn't doing too well before actor Joe Pesci introduced them to boy-wonder songwriter Bob Gaudio, who became the quartet's keyboardist. The Four Seasons took off, spinning song hits like "Sherry," "Big Girls Don't Cry," "Walk Like a Man," "Can't Take My Eyes Off You," "My Eyes Adored You," "Grease," and many more. Their story inspired the Broadway hit *Jersey Boys*, which won the Tony for Best Musical and whose movie version was directed by Clint Eastwood. John Lloyd Young got to reprise his role as Valli, for which he'd also won a Tony Award.

Valpolicella is a celebrated Veneto wine combing corvina, rondinella, and molinara grapes. It's a light- to medium-bodied red, best at one to three years of age. However, producers with an eye on high-end international markets increasingly make more complex wines with bigger concentrations of fruit and enhanced "mouthfeel."

Bardolino, a light dry red, is made from the same grape varieties as Valpolicella and is grown on the southeastern shore of Lake Garda near the town of Bardolino. Valpolicella means valley of many cellars.

Giorgio Vasari (1511-1574), a successful Renaissance painter and architect—the Uffizi in Florence, etc.—likely never imagined he'd be far better remembered as a biographer of other artists than as one himself. His massive *Lives of the Most Eminent Painters, Sculptors, and Architects*, dedicated to his patron Cosimo de Medici, was a success partly because it's entertaining as well as informative. Unfortunately, when facts on a given subject were few, Vasari tended to substitute hearsay. Also, his bias toward Italian and particularly Tuscan art is notable. Even so, his book was the first large-scale attempt at modern historiography and was extremely influential.

Besides his biographical portraits, Vasari analyzes three periods of artistic endeavor: the outstanding classical era, the Dark Ages when art served religious dogma, and the classical-inspired excellence of the Renaissance. His book's much expanded second edition appeared in 1550, and an English translation appeared in the 1850s.

Vatican City is the world's smallest country, with 108.7 acres and a population of about 900, all male. The popes ruled much of central Italy until the mid-1800s; in 1870 the pope also lost Rome and withdrew to the Vatican in seclusion and protest. In 1929 an agreement was reached and Vatican City became independent. The papacy also controls several churches in Rome, a radio station on Italian soil, and the papal summer residence at Castel Gandolfo.

The pope is his country's head of state and holds executive, legislative, and judicial powers. Vatican City has its own small army-police force: the "Swiss Guard," some 150 strong, established in 1506. Their Renaissance-style costumes were designed in 1914, not, as rumor has it, by Michelangelo.

Vatican City also has its own newspaper, stamps, currency, an abbreviated railroad, and the Bank of the Holy Ghost.

The Vatican Library, in terms of its contents' value, may be the greatest library in the world. It began under Pope Nicholas V (1447-1455), formerly private librarian to Cosimo de Medici in Florence. Over the centuries, various notables helped enlarge the collection, including the Swedish monarch Christina who abdicated and moved to Rome. The library comprises 1.6 million books, 150,000 manuscripts, 30,000 medals and coins, and 20,000 art objects dating back to ancient Egypt—this is apart from the extensive Vatican Museums. The library also contains the Vatican archives of the popes' confidential documents and correspondence, accessible up to those of 1920 to scholars. The rumor that the library has major pornographic holdings has repeatedly been denied.

Venice, the city of watery boulevards, is unique in the world. Comprising 120 islands, 170 canals, and over 400 bridges, it started as a humble town of fishermen and salt traders. By the ninth century it was a proud, independent political state that eventually dominated the Mediterranean's economy through commerce and conquest. Its power and glory continued until the nineteenth century and Napoleon.

Today Venice is a cherished tourist destination whose popularity and geography threaten its future. Upkeep is constant and considerable: canals must be dredged to remove the accretion of mud and silt, while buildings require repair and restoration against the leaning and crumbing caused by shifting foundations and dank air. The city's biographer Elizabeth Horodowich notes, "No piece of Venice can be allowed to sit for too long before nature begins to eat away at the built environment."

Venice, California. Tobacco millionaire Abbott Kinney's Venice of America opened in 1905, south of Santa Monica—it remained independent until 1926, when it was merged into Los Angeles. The beach resort boasted miles of canals, 24 imported gondoliers, arched colonnades inspired by the Doge's palace, bowling alleys, an aquarium, club house, theatre, dance pavilion, casino, and a 1,200-foot-long pleasure pier. Weekends, the town of 10,000 often drew 50,000 to 100,000 visitors.

In 1929 L.A.'s municipal government decided to pave over most of the canals, and in ensuing decades Venice became neglected to the extent that by the '50s it was often dubbed Slum by the Sea. Orson Welles's 1958 *Touch of Evil* was filmed there; Venice stood in for a seedy Mexican border town.

Venice has since more or less cleaned up its act, and is best known for its pedestrians-only, carnival-like

Ocean Front Walk—two and a half miles of buskers, vendors, artists, roller skaters, fortune-tellers, and assorted exhibitionists.

The Venice Film Festival is the world's oldest, founded in 1932 by Count Giuseppe Volpi. It takes place in late August or early September on the island of the Lido and is part of the Venice Biennale, a prestigious international cultural multi-event (started in 1895) that also embraces art, architecture, music, theatre, and dance. The film festival's major awards include the Golden Lion, the Silver Lion, and sometimes a Special Lion and the Coppa Volpi.

Giuseppe Verdi, sometimes half-jokingly translated as Joe Green, was the greatest Italian composer of operas. Born near Parma, Verdi (1813-1901) was no overnight success. The Conservatoire of Milan rejected him in 1832 and for years his father-in-law supported him. In 1838 his first daughter died, in 1839 his wife died, and his 1840 opera *King for a Day* was such a flop that Verdi was ready to abandon music but for his contractual obligations. In 1842 he experienced his first big success with *Nabucco*. Then came *Rigoletto*, *Il Trovatore*, *La Traviata*, *The Masked Ball*, *The Force of Destiny*, *Don Carlos*, *Aida*—commissioned to celebrate the opening of the Suez Canal—and more. Verdi's final opera, *Falstaff*, based on Shakespeare's *The Merry Wives of Windsor*, was written in 1893.

The very rich Verdi left his entire estate to a retirement home for indigent singers, composers, and musicians that still functions today.

Verona has its Shakespearean associations, as in *Two Gentlemen of…* and *Romeo and Juliet*. It's also the second biggest city in the Veneto region, after Venice, founded by the Romans in 89 BCE and boasting more Roman ruins than any city in Italy but Rome. Most spectacularly, this includes the Arena, the world's third-largest Roman amphitheatre, after the Colosseum and that of Capua, near Naples. Its original oval dimensions were 380 feet by 470 feet, with 74 entrances (80 for the Colosseum). The structure seated some 22,000 spectators, back when there were far fewer people. Like the Colosseum, the Arena was diminished over the centuries by those using it to provide construction material for other buildings, usually churches. What remains is still awesome, in the true sense of the word.

Geronimo Veroneo may not or might have been the architect or one of the architects of the Taj Mahal, built between ca. 1632 and ca. 1654. Veroneo was living in Agra at the time, and Shah Jahan did employ Italian artists to teach his craftsmen how to inlay marble with semi-precious stones for the mausoleum dedicated to his favorite wife. An Iberian monk who journeyed to Agra in 1642 to try and ransom another monk kept captive by the Muslim rulers wrote, "The (Taj Mahal's) architect was a Venetian, by name Geronimo Veroneo." Other sources stated Veroneo was one of three architects, besides a Persian and a Frenchman. Still others declared that Veroneo designed or helped design the intricate inlaid mosaics of that incomparable and enduring monument.

Veronese's blues. Paolo Caliari (1528-1588), better known as Paolo Veronese after his hometown of Verona, was a supreme colorist, most often associated with paintings of religious myth. Like any apprentice, he had to learn to grind pigments, but reveled in the process. A color sometimes called Veronese green is less a shade than a technique—microscopic testing has revealed layers of copper resinate, verdigris, lead white, and lead-tin yellow.

Veronese's signature color was blue, and he boldly set blue against orange without it seeming loud. Basic blues of his day included: azurite, which had a greenish tinge; smalt, a by-product of glass blowing that reacted with linseed oil and altered the color after 50 or 100 years (unknown to do so at the time); indigo, cheaper than smalt but longer-lasting; and ultramarine, made of crushed lapis lazuli from what is now Afghanistan, so expensive that the amount used in a painting—often for intense heavenly skies—was stipulated in the contract.

Over the centuries, some critics would praise Veronese's overcast or "subtle grey skies," unaware that the smalt had rendered them so and that Veronese, after whom a vivid shade of blue is named, only painted glowing blue skies.

Gianni Versace was born (1946-1997) in Reggio Calabria, the son of a female dressmaker whose older son was Santo and daughter was Donatella. Gianni studied architecture before moving to Milan to pursue fashion design. In 1978 he founded the company that would employ several relatives, and began creating in-demand clothes, accessories, fragrances, makeup, and home furnishings. He also designed for theatre, film, and concert tours; friends with Elton John, Cher, Sting, Eric Clapton, and Madonna, Versace was the first designer to link fashion and music in a big way.

Versace, whom *Forbes* magazine declared the most financially successful Italian designer ever, was shot to death outside his Miami mansion in 1997, motive still unknown. As of 2015 there were over 80 Versace boutiques around the world.

Vespa. "It looks like a wasp!" (Sembra una vespa!), exclaimed Enrico Piaggio upon first viewing his company's new MP6 scooter in 1946. After World War II Piaggio, the company founded by father Rinaldo Piaggio in Pontedera, was forbidden to manufacture aircraft. The focus shifted to affordable transportation. Demand built steadily, then went international via the movie hit *Roman Holiday* (1953), in which Audrey Hepburn hopped aboard Gregory Peck's

Vespa. In time there was a full line of Vespas and it became but one of seven companies owned by Piaggio. In 2004 Vespa introduced a gas-electric hybrid.

Villa is an Italian word meaning a big country house with its own grounds. It meant the same in ancient Rome, but with the rooms arranged around a courtyard. In time the word went international, usually but not always denoting a countryside or seaside home, typically more than one storey. With its Italian association, the word retains a glamour not necessarily justified by its usage. For example in England a villa is simply a detached or semi-detached house in a residential district.

"Villa" is frequently used in the names of upscale or wannabe hotels and motels. A Palm Springs, California, motel co-owner explains, "It sounds Continental if we say Villa, but without the inference of France and overpricing or Spain and run-down. Villa sounds Italian, so it's exotic but comfortable…glamorous but friendly. It's upscale but not intimidating. You know, Italian."

Villa of the Monsters is the nickname of the Villa Palagonia, a few miles from Palermo, Sicily, near Bagheria. Built for the hunchbacked Francesco Gravina, prince of Palagonia, by architect Tommaso Napoli in 1715, it's a wildly excessive and negative Baroque must-see-to-believe. The outer walls were ornamented with some 200—60 remain—statues of dwarves, deformed people, monsters, and monstrous animals. Legend had it that many of the depictions were caricatures of the prince's wife's lovers. The building's interior features numerous distorting wall mirrors that make visitors appear hunchbacked.

Luchino Visconti (1906-1976) was complex and contradictory. A count from a noble, rich family in Milan, he was a Marxist and openly gay yet also sexist and old-fashioned. In control of his movies, he never worked in Hollywood, which offered to film his *Death in Venice* (1971) if he would change the male protagonist's love object from a youth to a girl. Visconti directed handsome actors of all sexual stripes, from Alain Delon, Farley Granger, and Burt Lancaster to Helmut Berger, a final "discovery" who starred in three of his later films, including as the gay Bavarian monarch *Ludwig* (1972). A patron of the arts and a strong cultural presence in his day, Visconti also worked on the stage and directed operas starring Maria Callas and others.

> *Ossessione* (Obsession) is a 1943 Visconti movie based on James M. Cain's novel *The Postman Always Rings Twice* (filmed by Hollywood in 1946), to which the filmmaker didn't hold the rights. The Fascists banned and destroyed *Ossessione*, but Visconti had kept a

> duplicate negative, from which all subsequent copies were made. Due to the rights situation, *Ossessione* was blocked from release outside Italy until 1976. In 1976 film critic Vincent Canby wrote that comparing Visconti's version with Hollywood's was like comparing *La Traviata* with a McDonald's commercial.

Monica Vitti (*née* Maria Luisa Ceciarelli in 1931) became a star via Michelangelo Antonioni's now-classic early-'60s films *L'avventura* (*The Adventure*), *La Notte* (*The Night*), *L'ecclisse* (*The Eclipse*), and *Il Desserto Rosso* (*The Red Desert*). A modern yet vulnerable Northern-style blonde, Monica became a symbol of both social change and auteurial expression. Her looks were sometimes compared to Barbra Streisand's but Vitti's international projects—like the comic-strip-inspired *Modesty Blaise* (1966)—and several of her post-Antonioni movies fared poorly, and the actress, active from 1954-1991, faded into cherished memory.

Antonio Vivaldi (1678-1741), best known for his epic composition *The Four Seasons*, created some 400 concertos, more than 90 operas, 73 sonatas, and 23 symphonies. Works of his are still being discovered! Born in Venice, he became a priest but due to his asthma didn't have to perform religious duties. Rather, he dwelt on composing and conducting. Vivaldi developed the three-movement concerto format of fast-slow-fast and contrasted solo instruments with the rest of an orchestra.

Yet when he died in Vienna, to which he moved in 1740, his passing went unnoticed. A pauper, he was buried, like Mozart, in an anonymous communal grave. His music went on to influence many musicians, particularly Johann Sebastian Bach.

Alan Alda's 1981 movie *The Four Seasons* made clever use of Vivaldi's eponymous work in its soundtrack.

Alessandro Volta (1745-1827). Volts and voltage were named after the Como-born physics professor who in 1792 discovered that interaction between two metals submerged in a liquid salty substance produced electricity. By 1799 Volta had created a "voltaic" pile—an electrical battery comprising alternating silver and zinc discs immersed in salty water. This revolutionary discovery yielded honors from London's Royal Society, a pension from Napoleon, and chairmanship of the University of Pavia's department of (!) philosophy. Volta is buried in a Roman-style mausoleum by Lake Como.

"The Wedding Cake" is the nickname given the enormous white-marble, very decorated memorial to King Victor Emmanuel II, who died in 1878. Begun in 1885, the monument was inaugurated in 1911, the 50-year anniversary of Italian unity. Its style is Greco-Roman, with umpteen columns, statues, stairways, and a huge equestrian statue of V.E. atop a huge base, at the foot of which is Italy's Tomb of the Unknown Soldier. Within the curvilinear monument—also irreverently known as The Typewriter or The Denture—are museums dedicated to Italian emigration and unification.

Victor Emmanuel went from king of Sardinia to a national king in 1861 partly because he was the peninsula's only native ruler at the time, plus his dynasty, the House of Savoy, was relatively popular. In 1861 Florence became the national capital, but after the pope lost Rome in 1870 the capital moved there.

A flagrant womanizer, Victor Emmanuel, a married man and father of six legitimate children, in 1847 began a relationship with a 14-year-old girl whom he much later married. Despite the grandiose Victor Emmanuel II Monument, he is buried in Rome's Pantheon.

Lina Wertmuller. Only a handful of women have been nominated for the Academy Award for Best Director, and none won until 2010. The first nominated was Wertmuller (born 1928), whose father had some Teutonic ancestors—as did director-aristocrat Luchino Visconti.

An assistant director to Federico Fellini on his classic *8½* (1962), which inspired the much-later Broadway musical (and its movie version) *Nine*, Wertmuller made her directorial bow in 1963 but broke through with a 1972 hit, *The Seduction of Mimi*.

Seven Beauties (1975), which she also wrote, finally opened the Academy's door to female directors.

Edith Wharton, the Pulitzer Prize-winning novelist best known for *Ethan Frome*, *The Age of Innocence*, and *The House of Mirth*, spent four months in Italy in 1903. The result was an essay collection titled *Italian Villas and Their Gardens*, one of the first books to dwell on Italian garden architecture and a significant influence on a generation of landscape architects. When Audrey Hepburn hosted the 1990 TV series *Gardens of the World* she declared herself a longtime admirer of the book, its author, and Italian gardens in particular because "They're not just for show or for privacy. There's an art to them… they're like spas for the soul."

Guy Williams was born Armand (nickname Armando) Catalano in 1924 and grew up in New York City's Little Italy. The handsome guy became a model, which led to acting, but only bit parts in movies. Williams became a star on the small screen, first in Disney's *Zorro*, which aired from 1957 to 1961 and was a major hit in Latin America, then on *Lost in Space* (1965-1968), which was to have been titled *Space Family Robinson.* Williams played Professor John Robinson and was first-billed but grew disenchanted when the series' focus shifted from the family to the small son, the robot, and the nefarious Professor Smith.

Post-TV, Guy Williams landed few movie roles and in 1979 moved to Buenos Aires, Argentina, which he'd visited in 1973, surprised and delighted to discover his popularity there. Guy gave up acting and lived off his investments and stock-market portfolio, and in 1977 toured South America with a circus he founded that featured a national fencing champion—Zorro was of course a swashbuckling swordsman himself. A self-admitted loner, Williams was found dead in his high-end apartment in Bs. As. in 1989.

Tennessee Williams. When *The Rose Tattoo* opened in 1951, some critics said it was Williams's happiest, and only happy, play so far. A bawdy comedy with its share of drama and heartache, it followed Tennessee's visit in the late 1940s to Italy and was influenced "by the vitality, humanity, and love of life expressed by the Italian people…I have felt more hopeful about human nature as a result of being exposed to the Italians." For the screen version, he insisted an Italian play the Italian—so Anna Magnani won a lead Academy Award, the first Italian performer to do so.

In the '60s Williams wrote a rare novel, *The Roman Spring of Mrs. Stone*, about a middle-aged American actress in Rome who becomes entangled with an abusive local gigolo—enacted none too well by Warren Beatty. Williams' closest of his romantic partners was an Italian American Frank Merlo, who died prematurely of cancer.

Wine. The ancient Cretans named Italy Enotria, the land of wine. Italy is still one of the world's leading wine producers, especially northern regions like Tuscany, Piedmont, Lombardy, and the Veneto. There exist more than 1,000 varieties of wine-producing Italian grapes, and methods for planting, training, and pruning vines vary significantly.

Besides regular bars, Italy is home to the osteria or hostaria, a tavern or wine shop which sells wine by the glass and serves a limited selection of home-type foods, usually listed on a blackboard. The atmosphere is relaxed, the food is light. An enoteca is a posher wine bar that serves wine by the bottle and may offer more complex food on its menu.

> Italian law classifies domestic wines into four categories, the fourth being humble VDT (vino da tavola, table wine). Third is ITG, for Typical Geographic Location—some 120 wines qualify. Second is DOC—Denomination of Controlled Origin—311 wines meet government

> standards and are guaranteed to have been produced in particular areas. Tops is DOCG—Denomination of Controlled and Guaranteed Origin, which meets DOC specifications and has passed a blind quality tasting. Only 36 wines currently attain this high standard.

The Women's World Cup was instituted in 1991 and like the men's version plays out every four years, most recently in 2015 in Canada. As with the men's Cup, the German team is as good as it gets. Unlike the men's, Italy and Brazil have yet to win. The women's Cup has delivered some major surprises—the first five Women's World Cup winners were the United States, Norway, Germany, Germany, and Japan. American soccer star and Olympic gold medalist Megan Rapinoe declares, "The Women's World Cup was long overdue and is as exciting and relevant as what is still called the World Cup.

"It offers an alternative to the entrenched national teams of the male competition. There's more variety and room for any good players and teams to reach the top."

World's tallest.... Oddly, few people outside Italy have heard of the Mole Antonelliana, for a time the world's tallest fully-accessible building. A mole is a structure of monumental proportions. This one from a distance resembles a sagging pyramid with a tall spire (it also recalls the Shwe-Dagon Pagoda in Rangoon/Yangon). In 1863 Alessandro Antonelli was hired by Turin's Jewish community, which had full civil rights since 1848, to design a synagogue in what was then a united Italy's capital (in 1864 the capital moved to Florence). But the architect kept adding height and requiring more money and time, until construction halted in 1869.

The city purchased the unfinished building in 1878. It opened in 1889, 550' tall (168 meters). The same year, Paris saw completion of the Eiffel Tower (986'/301 meters), which claimed the world's-tallest title until the Empire State Building. The Mole Antonelliana housed the Museum of the Risorgimento from 1908-1938 and in 1961—unification's 100-year anniversary—an elevator was installed with a panoramic view of Turin and the Alps. Today this architectural symbol of Turin houses the Museo Nazionale del Cinema, the world's tallest museum, and remains the tallest masonry building in Europe and the tallest brick building in the world.

Yankee Doodle. Why did he stick a feather in his hat and call it macaroni? Few people in mid-eighteenth-century England were acquainted with macaroni, but being Italian, it was looked down on by most Brits.

Thus, a 1700s Englishman who dressed, spoke, or behaved in an affected manner was nicknamed macaroni. The "Yankee Doodle" lyric by a UK surgeon, Richard

Shuckburgh, implied that American colonists were naïve and unconcerned enough to believe adorning one's hat with a feather labeled one a macaroni. The song, sung by the British army, became unexpectedly popular in the American colonies at the time of the revolutionary war. Possibly proving Dr. Shuckburgh's point.

Zabaglione, aka zabaione. Imagine an egg-based whipped dessert that's creamy and sweet but given to someone with a cold or other ailment to "build their strength." True! Healthy people also eat it, as a dessert or a sauce for cake or fruit. It dates back to at least 1570 and is basically egg yolks, sugar, sometimes cinnamon, and dry or sweet Marsala or vin santo, and must be eaten as soon as it's made or it may collapse. Variations include Chilled Zabaglione with Berries, usually raspberries or blueberries, and Chocolate Zabaglione. So build, already.

Jimmy Zappalorti (1945-1990). The Zappalorti family of Staten Island were in the stained glass business, their clients including over 30 local churches and others in Canada and the West Coast. Youngest son Jimmy was gay and a disabled Navy veteran. He worked at the family trade, planted trees, cleared debris, was gentle, quiet, and known as a good neighbor. When two young toughs followed him home from a deli and demanded all his money, he threw his wallet into some weeds. That enraged 20-year-old Michael Taylor, a verbally abusive homophobe with a criminal record. With a hunting knife he repeatedly and fatally stabbed Jimmy. An additional wound may have been inflicted by his accomplice Philip Sarlo, 26.

Thanks to gay activists and Jimmy's family, the media took notice, eventuating in the first anti-hate-crimes legislation (bearing Jimmy's name) enacted in New York State. Sarlo died in prison in 1997 and Taylor, known as an unruly prisoner, was denied parole in 2012 but will seek it again in October 2016. Elder brother Robert Zappalorti authored a 2014 book about Jimmy titled *Stained Glass Windows*. The street the family lived on has been renamed Jimmy Zappalorti Lane.

Lena Zavaroni (1963-1999) still holds the British record as the youngest singer to place an album in the Top Ten— "Ma! He's Making Eyes at Me"—in 1974, aged ten. Her father played guitar and accordion, her mother sang, and her grandfather had emigrated from Genoa. The Scottish-born "Little Girl with the Big Voice" went on to host *Lena Zavaroni and Music* on BBC-TV in 1979, followed by a 1980-1982 series, *Lena*, and she released several more albums.

Reportedly battling anorexia nervosa since age 13, Zavaroni married in 1989—it lasted 18 months—the same year her mother died of a tranquilizer overdose and a fire destroyed all Lena's show business mementos. Suffering extreme depression, anorexia, and drug dependency, Lena underwent neurosurgery ten years later but died of complications at 35, weighing less than 70 pounds (32 kilograms). Her music lives on.

Zucchini is the plural of zucchino, the diminutive of zucco, meaning gourd. This small member of the gourd family was brought to Europe from the Americas and is tastier than bigger marrows. Zucchini can of course be stuffed—with a melting cheese like mozzarella and herbs and, say, anchovies, or with ricotta, herbs, and…you name it!

Zucchini flowers, frequently sold attached to immature marrows, may be fried lightly in butter, folded into frittatas, or battered and deep-fried. Roman frittatas are made with sliced rounds of zucchini that have been cooked in olive oil.

Zuccotto hasn't achieved the international popularity of another Italian dessert, tiramisu. Give it time….the dome-shaped cake is a Florentine specialty that needs no baking. A big bowl is lined with slabs of liqueur-soaked pound or sponge cake, then packed in with chestnuts or hazelnuts, candied fruits, almonds, and whipped cream, topped with more cake and dusted with confectioner's sugar. In bakeries it's increasingly covered over with a rich chocolate glaze. If the calories don't scare you off, ask for Zuccotto alla Cioccolata!

Zuppa Inglese, or English Soup, is the fanciful name for the richer Italian version of English Trifle that typically comprises sponge or pound cake slices, raspberry or sour cherry jam, orange liqueur or dark rum, chocolate as well as vanilla pastry cream, heavy whipping cream, and a garnish of fresh raspberries plus chocolate shavings. Makes the British original look healthy and low-cal by comparison!